T0076988

WORD
BIBLICAL
THEMES

General Editor
David A. Hubbard

Old Testament Editor
John D. W. Watts

New Testament Editor
Ralph P. Martin

WORD
BIBLICAL
THEMES

---

1 and 2 Chronicles

RODDY L. BRAUN

To the good people of
Our Savior Lutheran Church
Arlington, Virginia

In appreciation for twelve years of our ministry together.

"I thank my God in all my remembrance of you,
always in every prayer of mine for you all
making my prayer with joy, thankful for your
partnership in the gospel from the first day
until now." (Philippians 1:3–5 RSV)

ZONDERVAN ACADEMIC

1 and 2 Chronicles
Copyright © 1991 by Word, Incorporated

Requests for information should be addressed to:
Zondervan, *3900 Sparks Dr. SE, Grand Rapids, Michigan 49546*

ISBN 978-0-310-11579-3 (softcover)

Library of Congress Cataloging-in-Publication Data

Braun, Roddy.
    1 and 2 Chronicles: Roddy Braun.
       p. cm.
    Includes bibliographical references and index.
    ISBN 978-0-849-90790-6
    1. Bible. O.T. Chronicles—Criticism, interpretation, etc. I. Bible. O.T. Chronicles.
English. Braun. 1990. II. Title. III. Title: 1 and 2 Chronicles. IV. Series.
    BS1345.2.B72 1991AA
    222'.606—dc2   90-36380

Unless otherwise noted, all Scripture quotations are from the author's translation. Scripture quotations marked RSV are taken from the Revised Standard Version of the Bible. Copyright © 1952 [2nd edition 1971] by the Division of Christian Education of the National Council of the Churches of Christ in the United States of America. Used by permission. All rights reserved.

Any internet addresses (websites, blogs, etc.) and telephone numbers in this book are offered as a resource. They are not intended in any way to be or imply an endorsement by Zondervan, nor does Zondervan vouch for the content of these sites and numbers for the life of this book.

No part of this publication may be reproduced, stored in a retrieval system, or transmitted in any form or by any means—electronic, mechanical, photocopy, recording, or any other—except for brief quotations in printed reviews, without the prior permission of the publisher.

Printed in the United States of America

HB 06.03.2022

CONTENTS

FOREWORD

Finding the great themes of the books of the Bible is essential to the study of God's Word, and to the preaching and teaching of its truths. But these themes or ideas are often like precious gems; they lie beneath the surface and can only be discovered with some difficulty. The large commentaries are useful in this discovery process, but they are not usually designed to help the student trace the important subjects within a given book of Scripture.

The Quick-Reference Bible Topics meet this need by bringing together, within a few pages, all of what is contained in a biblical volume on the subjects that are thought to be most significant to that volume. A companion series to the Word Biblical Commentary, these books seek to distill the theological essence of the biblical books as interpreted in the more technical series and to serve it up in ways that will enrich the preaching, teaching, worship, and discipleship of God's people.

The books of Chronicles present an alternative retelling of the story which began with Adam and culminated with

David and Solomon's heirs in Jerusalem. Roddy L. Braun has extracted the most important themes from that story which give it relevance and meaning for us. This volume is sent forth in the hope that it will contribute to the vitality of God's people, renewed by the Word and the Spirit and ever in need of renewal.

Southern Baptist Theological
   Seminary
Louisville, Kentucky

John D. W. Watts
Old Testament Editor
Word Biblical Commentary
Quick-Reference Bible Topics

INTRODUCTION

Casual readers of the Old Testament are prone to make two common errors in their approach to the Old Testament. First, in their study of the prophets they tend to treat the prophets' words as completely theological and ignore the historical background of the book. Secondly, in studying what we usually term the historical books, they concern themselves only with the historical aspect of the work and ignore its theological message. In both cases, the result is a misreading of the divinely intended message.

The study of Chronicles presents a unique opportunity to see the theological side of what we usually call a historical writing. We have in the books of Samuel-Kings the commonly acknowledged source which the Chronicler used in writing his own "history" of Israel. This permits us to view in much clearer perspective the alterations, deletions, and additions which the author has introduced into his text. While the possibility of error must be acknowledged with regard to smaller changes, and the possibility of textual difficulties is always possible, we are on firmer ground in appraising the larger additions which the Chronicler has made to his work. Accordingly, in this book primary attention will be directed to material found in those sections of Chronicles which have no parallel in Samuel-Kings.

While it has in the past been considered scholarly orthodoxy to view the two books of Chronicles and the books of Ezra and Nehemiah as coming from the pen of the same author, this theory has faced serious criticism of late. Accordingly, in this work Ezra and Nehemiah will be left aside. Readers wishing to explore that relationship in more detail may test the unity or disunity of this literary corpus by considering the themes presented in this book and comparing them with the text of Ezra and Nehemiah.

Among critical scholars, two larger sections of 1 Chronicles are often denied to the Chronicler: chapters 1-9 and chapters 23-27. Since the inclusion of these chapters in the material of this book would not alter substantially its contents (the themes of "all Israel" and of priests and Levites found there are well-represented elsewhere in Chronicles), minimal attention has been paid to them in this work.

Years ago, Gerhard von Rad saw in some of the speeches in Chronicles certain characteristics which led him to define these speeches as "Levitical sermons." In recent years, some attention has been given to the attempt to define the literary type which is of the essence of the book of Chronicles. One term that has been used in that connection is midrash, a name applied to ancient Jewish commentaries upon a portion of Scripture. The midrashim (pl.) are of a nonlegal and often fanciful nature. While such attempts are of interest, and a similarity in the manner in which such sermons and works have dealt with a biblical text is present, no meaningful breakthrough can be said to have occurred in Chronicles studies, and the matter has not been pursued here. Chronicles is what it is—a writer or writers, believed by adherents of church and synagogue to have been working under divine inspiration, pondering another text which he would have accepted as authoritative and retelling that story with particular emphasis upon matters which he considered crucial for the people of his own day. Whether that process be called sermonizing or a reflection of devotional piety, the result is the same. The books of Chronicles are a message to people based upon an earlier message, which the later author has adapted to his particular situation and to his understanding of God's deeds with his people. Readers of the Bible today follow the same process in applying the text to their own situation. It is this same task of interpreting the biblical message for a new audience in a later day that falls to preachers and teachers of church and synagogue as they seek to make God's Word relevant to the people whom they serve.

There is much we do not know about Chronicles. We do not know who the writer or writers were, nor when the book was written, or to whom. Earlier opinions which placed at least the great bulk of the book as late as 300 B.C. or even later appear to be yielding to others which place the work earlier, even as early as the Exile.[1] Many emphases of the book would be most appropriate in the period surrounding the building of the second temple, which was dedicated in 515 B.C.

Within the canon of the English Bible, the books of Chronicles immediately follow the books of Kings and precede the books of Ezra and Nehemiah, and are usually termed "history." However, in the Hebrew canon Chronicles is the last book of the Bible, a position which it seems to have had in Jesus' day according to the reference in Matthew 23:25. (The last martyr to whom he refers seems certainly to be the Zechariah whose murder is recorded in 2 Chronicles 24:20–21.) It is a puzzling anomaly that in the Hebrew canon Chronicles is *preceded* by Ezra-Nehemiah, a book or books which certainly deal with a later historical period. As such, both are parts of the third portion of the Jewish canon usually referred to with the rather nondescript term, "the Writings," while, for example, the books of Samuel and Kings are found in that part of the canon called the Former Prophets, which reached canonical status some time earlier. This third portion of the Hebrew canon was apparently still only loosely organized in New Testament times, where it is referred to as "the Psalms," after its most prominent part. It would remain for the rabbinic council meeting in Jamnia in 90 A.D. to define clearly the contents of this last part of the Hebrew canon. At any rate, however, the term "history" is not an appropriate designation for writings in which theological interpretation and prophetic preachment is so prominent.

The following outline of the two books, which recognizes the important position of 1 Chronicles 22-29 in unifying two parts of the work often pitted against each other, may be helpful to the reader:

I. Genealogical Prologue, 1 Chr 1-9
II. The United Monarchy
   A. The David History, 1 Chr 10-21
   B. Transitional Unit, 1 Chr 22-29
   C. The Solomon History, 2 Chr 1-9
III. The Divided Monarchy, 2 Chr 10-36

In this volume, translations are regularly my own, unless otherwise noted. Some effort has been made to remain as close to the Revised Standard Version as possible, except in the use of the Tetragrammaton, which has regularly been transliterated "Yahweh," and in other cases where clarity or precision demanded otherwise. Occasionally, a Hebrew word or grammatical term may appear in this volume. I hope that such terms will aid those who know at least some of the Hebrew language. For the readers unfamiliar with that language, I have sought to make the meaning clear within the context. I hope that I have succeeded. Where a reference is identified WBC 15, I am quoting from the translation of Raymond Dillard in his volume *2 Chronicles* in the Word Biblical Commentary, volume 15.

Roddy L. Braun
Our Savior Lutheran Church
Arlington, Virginia

1

THE GOD OF THE FATHERS

O Yahweh, the God of Abraham, Isaac, and Israel, our fathers, keep for ever such purposes and thoughts in the hearts of your people, and direct their hearts toward you. (1 Chr 29:18)

The Bible is first of all a book about God. Theology in all of its branches is words or study (Greek *logos*) about God (*theos*).

It is especially necessary to make this point at the beginning of a study of Chronicles, where it might be particularly easy to lose sight of that fact. Lengthy genealogies, the prominence of such topics as the temple, David and Solomon and Israel's other kings, and retribution (even *divine* retribution) can divert our attention from the God whom the inspired writer we shall call *the Chronicler* saw as the very center of his community's faith and life.

Chronicles is meant to be read in the context of the entire Old Testament story of God's dealings with his people. That is made apparent, first of all, from the first nine chapters of the work, in which "the story" is summarized by means of a lengthy genealogical prologue. (A New Testament writer, Matthew, will use the same means several centuries later to span the entire history of Israel from Abraham to Jesus; see Matt 1:1–17; also Luke 3:23–38.) The God with whom the books of Chronicles have to do is the Creator God and the God of all creation. His people reach all the way back to Adam, Enoch, Methusaleh, and Noah (1 Chr 1:1–4). They include all of the sons of Noah's son Shem, or the Semites as we know them today; and not only the Semitic peoples, but the descendants of Japheth and Ham (1 Chr 1:5–16), including Egyptians and Canaanites alike.

Israel's God is the God of Abraham, Isaac, *and* Ishmael (1 Chr 1:28), the progenitor of the Arab tribes. He is the God of Jacob/Israel *and* Esau/Seir, the father of the Edomites (1 Chr 1:34–54). He is the one and only God, as David will confess in his prayer, to whom belongs the kingdom, the power, and the glory, to whom belongs everything in heaven and on earth (1 Chr 29:10–13).

But in a special sense this God, who revealed his name and character to Moses as *Yahweh* (conventionally translated LORD), is the God of Abraham (1 Chr 1:28, 34), with whom he entered into a special covenant and through whose descendants he promised to bring blessing upon all the families of the earth (Gen 12:1–4).

Yahweh is the God of the fathers, or patriarchs—of Abraham, of his son Isaac, of Isaac's son Jacob (renamed *Israel* in Gen 35:10), and of the twelve tribes or subdivisions named after Jacob's twelve sons, to which the name *Israel* has come to be attached. The lengthy genealogies of 1 Chronicles 2–8, introduced with the simple "These are the Israelites: . . . ," spare no detail and make no compromise with the reader's patience or interest in establishing that point.

It is about this Yahweh as God of the fathers, God of Israel, that we read most frequently in the books of Chronicles.

David prays to him as "Yahweh, the God of our father Israel" (1 Chr 29:10). He is, in words that we read repeatedly, "the God of the fathers" (2 Chr 24:18, 24; 28:6, 9, 25), "the God of Abraham, Isaac, and Israel" (1 Chr 29:6), and most frequently simply "the God of Israel" (2 Chr 6:4; 7:11, 16; 13:5; 15:4, 13). It was he who chose David to be king over Israel forever (1 Chr 28:4), and upon the throne of whose kingdom Solomon would sit as king (1 Chr 29:23). Though he cannot be confined to an earthly temple, yet he has deigned to place his name in his house in Jerusalem, where rests the ark of his presence (1 Chr 28:2). It is before this God that the priests and Levites minister, and before whom his people Israel is to worship. It is he who speaks to his people by the mouth of his prophets (2 Chr 36:15). It is he, "the God of heaven," who will stir up the spirit of the Persian king Cyrus to release a captive remnant of "his people" to return to Jerusalem in Judah to build him a house (2 Chr 35:23).

Chronicles therefore is not summoning the people of its day to the service of a new deity, or even to new forms of service. The writer is urging them to take up again their loyalty to the God who long ago made them his people and who has dealt with them so faithfully in the past. He is summoning them to the same institutions which their fathers knew, and to the obedience of the same statutes which their fathers obeyed. In such a program they would find the blessing and prosperity which God desired for his people.

Christians, Jews, and Muslims alike are strong to emphasize the connection or relationship between this "God of the fathers," the God of the Hebrew Scriptures, and their own faith. The New Testament, for example, cannot be understood properly except in terms of its claim to be the fulfillment of the Old Testament. We have already referred to the tracing of Jesus' lineage to David and Abraham, and even beyond that to Adam and God.

The God of the Fathers   3

"Son of David" is a regular designation of the One who is viewed as the fulfillment of the Messianic promise to David (cf. Matt 1:1; Mark 10:47; Rom 1:3-4), and the charge brought against Jesus before Pilate was that he claimed to be the king of the Jews (Luke 23:3). The preaching of the apostolic age, as evidenced in the sermon of Stephen (Acts 7), tells the Old Testament story as a part of its own story. Jesus proclaims his own unity with that Father (John 10:30), and prays to him from the cross (Luke 23:34). The God who spoke to the fathers through the prophets "has in these last days spoken to us through a Son" (Heb 1:1-2). Thus a principle exemplified so early in Old Testament history continues to be a significant part of the message of the church.

2

THE TEMPLE

Now Solomon planned to build a temple for the name of Yahweh, and a royal palace for himself. . . . And Solomon sent word to Huram the king of Tyre: ". . . Behold, I am building a house for the name of Yahweh my God and dedicate it to him for the burning of incense of sweet spices before him, and for the continual offering of the showbread, and for burnt offerings morning and evening, on the sabbath and the new moons and the appointed feasts of Yahweh our God, as ordained for ever for Israel. The house which I am building will be great, for our God is greater than all gods. But who is able to build him a house, since heaven, even highest heaven, cannot contain him? Who am I to build a house for him, except as a place to burn incense before him?" (2 Chr 2:1, 3-6)

At the center of the books and of the concerns of Chronicles stands the temple. Sometimes the focus is on the temple per se, sometimes the concern is broadened to include the ministers and services of the temple. Sometimes these concerns are explicit; at other times they are partially obscured by the larger presentation of which they are a part, but of which they in fact stand at the heart. By way of example, 1 Chronicles 10-12 portrays the rise of David—but it will be the function of David, in company with Solomon, to build the temple. First Chronicles 23-27 deals principally with the priests and Levites, as do many other sections of Chronicles, but their function is the ministry of the temple. In 2 Chronicles 10-36 the post-Solomonic history of Israel is told, and we will show that the concept of retribution lies at the base of the Chronicler's presentation. However, that history also revolves around the temple.

The temple is central too, we might recall, in Deuteronomy (D) and the Deuteronomistic History (DH), that portion of the Old Testament showing marked similarities to Deuteronomy in vocabulary, style, and content and consisting of the books of Joshua, Judges, 1 and 2 Samuel, and 1 and 2 Kings.

Deuteronomy's insistence upon a single sanctuary, commonly understood as the Jerusalem temple, is well known (cf. Deut 12:1-14; 26:1-4). The narrative up to the erection of the temple by Solomon moves steadily if slowly and circuitously to that point. And the overwhelming significance of that event for the writer is clear not only from the amount of space devoted to its building and dedication (1 Kgs 6-8), but also from the length and content of the speeches placed on Solomon's lips by the author (1 Kgs 8:12-53, 54-61). It is also on the basis of their relationships to the Jerusalem temple that post-Solomonic kings of both Israel and Judah are judged; and the fate of the temple and its vessels constitutes a significant part of the narrative of the fall of Jerusalem (2 Kgs 24:13; 25:13-17).

As is often the case, however, the writer or writers of Chronicles, whom we without prejudice call "the Chronicler," often adopts and develops a principle enunciated earlier by D and DH in a much more consistent and thorough manner. (See especially the concept of "retribution" in chapter 6, and "rest" in chapter 9.) Israel's history from David and Solomon to the temple, and afterward to the fall of the nation, is told for the sake of the temple.

David and the temple

This perspective on Israel's history may not seem as clear with respect to David as it does to Solomon, even though many scholars have emphasized David's role in the construction of the temple (and in Chronicles in general) at the expense of Solomon. The first chapters of what we might call "The David History" (1 Chr 10–21) speak of David's rise to power in accordance with God's will and word and of Israel's unanimous consent to that rule (1 Chr 10–12). Yet the purpose for which David has been chosen as king by Yahweh is the building of the temple in conjunction with Solomon. The same kind of support—unanimous and enthusiastic—will be sought for Solomon by David and accorded him by "all Israel" (cf. 2 Chr 29, especially vv 23–25).

Following David's acclamation as king at Hebron by "all Israel" (2 Chr 11:1–3), David moves immediately to the conquest of Jerusalem, destined to be the site of Yahweh's temple (2 Chr 11:4–9). After the inclusion of a potpourri of lists (1 Chr 11:10–12:37), the purpose of which is to demonstrate the extent of David's popular support (1 Chr 12:38–40 [in Hebrew, these are verses 39–41]) by all Israel, attention turns immediately to the ark of the covenant, the centerpiece of the temple (1 Chr 13:1–14). The failure of this first mission, later explained as due to the failure of the Levites to carry the ark (1 Chr 15:2, 14–15), provides opportunity for the inclusion of assorted notices from 2 Samuel 5 highlighting

David's fame and family and portraying his victory in warfare (1 Chr 14:1-16; see especially verse 17, which is added by the Chronicler). The ark is clearly central again in chapters 15 and 16, with emphasis now—perhaps added by a later author—upon the various Levitical families and their tasks (1 Chr 15:4-24; 16:4-6). The ark is successfully delivered to Jerusalem (1 Chr 16:1-4) and properly cared for by its Levitical attendants, as is the tabernacle, which according to the Chronicler's presentation was left at Gibeon together with the altar of burnt offering (1 Chr 16:39-42; cf. 2 Chr 1:1-6). From Gibeon it will later be brought to Jerusalem to rejoin the ark (2 Chr 5:5).

With these arrangements taken care of, attention can begin to be focused upon the temple itself, and this is done in 1 Chronicles 17, the Chronicler's version of the dynastic oracle of 2 Samuel 7. Here it is affirmed that not David, but one of his sons, i.e., Solomon, will actually build the temple.[1]

This focus upon the temple appears to be interrupted by 1 Chronicles 18-20, which chapters recount various wars of David from 2 Samuel 8, 10, 12, and 21. The writer's reason for including these chapters is difficult to say. It may be that the author has simply repeated them "because they were there," or because he wished to show David's prowess, or to depict David as a bloody warrior unfit to build the temple (cf. 1 Chr 22:8). However, the Chronicler's own addition in 1 Chronicles 18:8 (see 2 Sam 8:8, where the reference to Solomon's use of the bronze is absent) points to the use of the spoils of battle in the manufacture of the temple vessels (cf. 2 Chr 5:1).

A more direct focus upon the temple is resumed in 1 Chronicles 21 (2 Sam 24), which concludes with David's sacrifice at and purchase of the threshing floor of Ornan the Jebusite. One may expect that the significantly higher price paid for the threshing floor (six hundred shekels of gold in

1 Chronicles 21:25 versus fifty shekels of silver in 2 Samuel 24:24) is indicative of the higher value which the Chronicler wishes to place upon property purchased for such a noble endeavor. At any rate, David's offering and prayer is in 1 Chronicles 21:26b answered directly by Yahweh with fire from heaven, and once again the Chronicler adds his own conclusion to the description of the events:

> At that time, when David saw that Yahweh had answered him at the threshing floor of Ornan the Jebusite, he made his sacrifices there. For the tabernacle of Yahweh, which Moses had made in the wilderness, and the altar of burnt offering were at that time in the high place at Gibeon; but David could not go before it to inquire of God, for he was afraid of the sword of the angel of Yahweh. Then David said, *"Here shall be the house of Yahweh God, and here the altar of burnt offering for Israel."* (1 Chr 21:28–22:1 RSV, italics added)

With the ark in Jerusalem, the Levites correctly ordered for its service, the location of the temple defined, and the property purchased, all appears to be in readiness for the work on the temple to begin.

There remain, however, several unanswered questions. Who is the divinely chosen successor of David, who will build the temple? How will it be built? Where will the funds come from? Who will tend its altars, maintain its ordinances, and lead its worship? These questions are addressed in 1 Chronicles 22–28.

The temple in 1 Chronicles 22–28

The answer provided to the first question is clearly, "Solomon." That is the primary apologetic thrust of

1 Chronicles 22, 28–29. (Chapters 23–27 are probably a later addition to the Chronicler's work, but are nevertheless directed primarily toward the functionaries of the temple, the Levites, ch 23; the priests, ch 24; the singers, ch 25; and the gatekeepers, ch 26. Only with chapter 27 does the author(s) turn to David's civil officials.) The writer in this important section demonstrates that Solomon was divinely chosen to build the temple in no less than three ways:[2]

1. By the use of the concept of rest (see pp. 105–13), he affirms that David could not build the temple, since he was a "man of war" and had "shed blood" (1 Chr 28:3; cf. 1 Chr 22:7). Solomon, whose very name means "peace," was the chosen temple builder, in whose days Yahweh would grant the peace, rest, and quietness which are the prerequisites for building his temple (1 Chr 22:9–10; 28:6–7).

2. In the Chronicler's account, both 1 Chronicles 22 and 28 show signs of being modeled upon a literary form for the induction of an individual into an office, and specifically upon such a form as is found in connection with Moses' induction of Joshua (Josh 1). There Joshua is inducted, for example, for the twofold task of conquering the land and apportioning it to the tribes of Israel (Deut 31:7–8; Josh 1:5–6). The book of Joshua in fact follows the same outline (conquest, chs 1–12; apportionment, chs 13–21; final matters, chs 22–24). In that context it then becomes most significant that the *only* task given to Solomon throughout chapters 22 and 28 is the construction of the temple:

Now, my son, may Yahweh be with you, so that you may succeed in building the house of Yahweh your God, as he has spoken concerning you. (1 Chr 22:11)

He will not fail you or forsake you, until all the work for the service of the house of Yahweh is finished. (1 Chr 28:10)

We may accordingly conclude that the reason that Chronicles modeled its presentation upon that of Joshua was to affirm that Solomon was the divinely chosen temple builder.

3. The Chronicler states in so many words that Yahweh chose (Heb. *bāḥar*) Solomon to be his son (1 Chr 28:6), to build his sanctuary (1 Chr 28:10) and his palace (1 Chr 29:1). No other Old Testament writer speaks of the election of any king after David!

We thus feel justified in maintaining that the principal purpose of 1 Chronicles 22, 28–29 is to designate Solomon as the divinely chosen temple builder.

In looking at these chapters, other themes and functions in relationship to the temple also become clear. Chief among these is the desire to indicate the profuse amount of materials provided by David and the people to construct the temple (22:1–5, 14–16; 28:14–18; 29:1–9). Prominent also is the desire to solicit and gain the support of Israel's leaders (28:1) and, indeed, of all Israel for both the temple project and for Solomon's leadership (29:6–10, 20–25).

Finally, the plans which David gave to Solomon for the temple (and, according to the present text, even the most detailed arrangements of the temple) are said to be plans from the hands of Yahweh himself (28:19; cf. verses 11–18). The total effect from reading these chapters, including the beautiful prayer attributed to David (29:10–19), is of a divinely ordained and defined project to be completed by King Solomon, to which David and all Israel respond with piety, joy, unanimity, generosity, and obedience, both to the Lord and to his chosen king and temple builder, Solomon.

Solomon and the temple

Chronicles begins the story of Solomon's reign with the account of Solomon's sacrifices at Gibeon, as does 1 Kings 3:4. But for the Chronicler this mention becomes the occasion for a Solomon-led procession of all Israel to the legitimate tent of meeting of Moses, where the legitimate bronze altar is located. This act of Solomon's faithfulness forms the backdrop against which Yahweh's first epiphany to Solomon occurs, culminating in Yahweh's assurance of unequaled wisdom, wealth, and honor for Solomon (2 Chr 1:7–13). Verses 14–17, which the Chronicler has transferred to this location from 1 Kings 10:26–29 in preference to the rather disparate account of 1 Kings 3:16–4:34, pictures fittingly and briefly Solomon's military strength and the wealth which followed.

With chapter 2, Chronicles moves directly to its concern for the temple. After his initial statement of the theme (v 1; Heb. 1:18*), Solomon gathers laborers for the task and arranges with Huram for the necessary materials (vv 1–15). But the Chronicler has used Solomon's correspondence with Huram not only to request timber for his building operations, but also through the rewriting of Solomon's message (vv 2–9) has included what amounts to both a confession of faith for Solomon and a significant statement of the purpose of the temple as seen by the writer (vv 3–5). Chronicles finds Kings' description of the temple as only a place of prayer inadequate, and supplements it strongly with references to sacrifice (vv 4, 6; Heb. vv 3, 5). Solomon's request for a craftsman to direct the more delicate work, which in Kings had stood quite alone (1 Kgs 7:13–14), is also made an original part of Solomon's request. Huram's reply is similarly altered. It concerns itself not only with the formalities of diplomatic correspondence as in Kings, but also adds as a kind of qualifying phrase to the statement concerning Solomon's wisdom the phrase "who will *build a temple*" for Yahweh and a royal palace for himself (2 Chr 2:12, Heb.

---

* In the Hebrew original text, it is 1:18. This abbreviated form will be used to indicate a variation in references.

v 11). As well, his reply outlines the arrangements made for Huramabi to serve as a craftsman for Solomon.[3]

The description of the temple's construction in 2 Chronicles 3-5 is largely parallel with 1 Kings 6-7, where the temple and its cult could hardly be more central. However, Chronicles adds in 5:11-13 a characteristic note concerning the participation of the Levitical singers in the ceremonies marking the transfer of the ark into the temple. Solomon's lengthy dedicatory prayer is likewise repeated almost verbatim (2 Chr 6:12-40 = 1 Kgs 8:22-53), although Chronicles alters the final verses to refer to the resting of the ark in its place and to the Davidic covenant rather than to the events of the Exodus. Immediate divine approval for Solomon's prayer is indicated by the appearance of fire from heaven, as in the case of David's prayer from the threshing floor of Ornan (2 Chr 7:1; cf. 1 Chr 21:26).

After the completion of the dedicatory feast, which the Chronicler has expanded to fourteen days (2 Chr 7:9; cf. 1 Kgs 8:66), the participation of the Levites is again noted (2 Chr 7:6), and a second appearance of Yahweh to Solomon is recorded (vv 11-22). Once again in this second discourse as framed by the Chronicler there is considerably more emphasis upon the temple than was the case in Kings (1 Kgs 9:2-9, where the dynastic emphasis is more central; cf. 1 Kgs 9:4-5). The significant insertion of the Chronicler in 2 Chronicles 7:12b-15 concentrates once again upon the temple as a place of sacrifice (v 12b) and upon the need for repentance and seeking Yahweh's face, all of which are clearly major themes for the author.[4]

After inclusion of much of the material of 1 Kings 9:10-28, where the Chronicler's literary sensitivities are apparent in that he has smoothed out much of the disparate character of the Kings account, the entire temple pericope reaches its conclusion for the Chronicler with Solomon's inauguration of the weekly, monthly, and annual sacrifices, together with the appointment of the divisions of the priests, Levitical singers, and gatekeepers as directed by David (2 Chr 8:12-15). The end of the temple narrative per se is reached in the following verse, also unique to Chronicles:

Thus was accomplished all the work of Solomon from the day the foundation of the house of Yahweh was laid until it was finished. So the house of Yahweh was completed. (2 Chr 8:16)

The account of the visit of the queen of Sheba and other closing notes climax the report of Solomon's prosperity, marking his God-pleasing reign (2 Chr 9:1-31).

The temple and the post-Solomonic kings

This central position of the temple is retained in the narrative of both the disruption of the kingdom under Rehoboam and the subsequent narrative of post-Solomonic kings. It was probably the Chronicler who first emphasized the role of Jeroboam in the schism. Chronicles notes that the priests and Levites in all Israel resorted to Rehoboam from wherever they lived because Jeroboam had dismissed them from serving as priests to Yahweh and appointed his own priests for the high places he had made (2 Chr 11:13-15).

And those who had set their hearts to seek Yahweh God of Israel came after them from all the tribes of Israel to Jerusalem to sacrifice to Yahweh. (2 Chr 11:16 RSV)

The Chronicler has reserved his definitive statement concerning the temple (and the dynasty), however, for the confrontation between Jeroboam and Abijah (2 Chr 13). In the speech placed in Abijah's mouth prior to his battle with

Jeroboam, the north is taken to task for its apostasy from the Davidic dynasty and from the worship in the legitimate temple in Jerusalem. However, the major emphasis both here and throughout the remainder of the work is clearly upon the temple. The north has forsaken Yahweh, the true God, since the people there have driven out Yahweh's priests, the Aaronites and Levites, and installed priests like other nations (2 Chr 13:9). Judah, on the other hand, has not forsaken Yahweh, for its people have the legitimate priesthood and keep the prescribed ceremonies (vv 9–11). The result is that Yahweh is *with* Judah, and her victory is assured. There is no evidence that the Chronicler ever deviated from this view of the unique significance of the Jerusalem sanctuary.

We may cover the remainder of 2 Chronicles in a more cursory way. This is so because, once the temple has been established and its significance also for Israel and Judah after the schism has been confirmed, its position, while no less significant, is often more in the background as the tale of retribution unwinds.

As a part of his reforms, Asa repairs the altar of Yahweh (2 Chr 15:8) and gathers the faithful from both north and south to Jerusalem for sacrifice and a covenant before the Lord (vv 8–15). Jehoshaphat proclaims a fast throughout Judah when threatened by a coalition of Moabites, Ammonites, and Meunites, and his prayer of faith "in the house of Yahweh, before the new court," is recorded (2 Chr 20:6–12) as well as Yahweh's answer there given by the prophet Jahaziel (vv 15–17).

The entire history of Joash revolved around the temple, for he was, according to Chronicles, raised secretly in the temple for six years during the reign of the wicked Athaliah by the wife of Jehoiada the priest (2 Chr 22:11–12), and then crowned as king in the temple with the support of the priests and Levites (2 Chr 23:1–21). He made plans to restore the house of the Lord, and reinstituted the tax levied by Moses (2 Chr 24:4–14). But after the death of Jehoiada, the princes of Judah and the king "forsook the house of Yahweh, the God of their fathers, and served the Asherim and the idols" (v 18), with the result that wrath came upon Judah and Jerusalem (vv 18, 23–24). Chronicles reports that during the reign of Amaziah, King Joash of Israel seized all the gold and silver and vessels found in the temple (2 Chr 25:24). Uzziah attempted to burn incense in the temple and became angry with the priests who attempted to dissuade him, and was stricken with leprosy in the temple as a result (2 Chr 26:16–20). Judah's fortunes seem to reach their nadir under the wicked King Ahaz, who shut the very doors of the house of Yahweh and built altars in every corner of Jerusalem and constructed high places throughout Judah (2 Chr 28:24–25).

It is left to King Hezekiah, for whom the Chronicler's devotion is almost boundless, to reverse this situation. It takes the Chronicler four lengthy chapters (2 Chronicles 29–32) to recount his heroics. The temple is cleansed, sin offerings are made for "all Israel" (29:20–24), and the Levites are set in their offices and consecrated. Chronicles concludes:

Thus the service of the house of Yahweh was restored. And Hezekiah and all the people rejoiced because of what God had done for the people; for the thing came about suddenly. (2 Chr 29:35b–36 RSV)

Invitations are then sent throughout Israel, from Beersheba to Dan, urging the people not to be recalcitrant, but to "yield themselves to Yahweh, and come to his sanctuary, which he has sanctified forever. . ." (2 Chr 30:8). And we are told that "some men from Asher, Manasseh, and Zebulun repented and came to Jerusalem" (2 Chr 30:11) to keep the feast. The resulting celebration is described in considerable detail (vv 13-27), and is obviously designed to parallel that of Solomon and his people upon the dedication of the temple (v 26).

When the celebration has been completed, high places are destroyed in both south and north (2 Chr 31:1), and the priests and Levites are again set in their courses and provision made for their upkeep (vv 2-19). This part of Hezekiah's reign is fittingly concluded with the Chronicler's own summary:

So Hezekiah did throughout all Judah. He did what was good, right, and faithful before Yahweh his God. And every work that he undertook in *the service of the house of God* and in accordance with the law and the commandments seeking his God, he did with all his heart, and prospered. (2 Chr 31:20-21)

Manasseh reversed many of Hezekiah's reforms, not only rebuilding the destroyed high places, but also building idolatrous altars to the host of heaven in the very temple courts and putting an idolatrous image in the temple (2 Chr 33:1-5). After his repentance it is reported that he cleansed the temple of the foreign idols "and restored the altar of the Lord" (vv 15-16).

Josiah's finding of the book of the law in the temple is, of course, well known (2 Kgs 22), and requires little supplementation by the Chronicler, except to note that the temple repairs were under the direction of the Levites (2 Chr 34:14-18). The story of Josiah's Passover, however, is liberally supplemented to emphasize both the magnitude of the offerings and the position of the Levites (2 Chr 35:1-19). Chronicles, like Kings, relates that Nebuchadnezzar carried part of the temple vessels to Babylon during the reign of Jehoiakim, and that after Zedekiah's rebellion the temple was burned and its treasuries and vessels were looted (2 Chr 36:7, 18-19).

It seems appropriate that the final verse of the book expresses its concern in terms of the temple:

Thus says Cyrus king of Persia, "Yahweh, the God of heaven, has given me all the kingdoms of the earth, and *he has charged me to build him a house at Jerusalem* which is in Judah. Whoever is among you of all his people, may Yahweh his God be with him. Let him go up." (2 Chr 36:23 RSV, emphasis added)

Priests and Levites

Closely associated with the temple are priests and Levites. We shall confine our attention to them to a few observations for three reasons: (1) The study is extremely complex, and no agreement has been reached on the subject. (2) While priests and Levites are prominent in Chronicles, many, if not most, of the passages dealing with the Levites in particular are often considered later additions to Chronicles. This is true, for example, of 1 Chronicles 1–9 (see especially 6:1–81; 9:10–34) and chapters 23–27, of which all but the last chapter is devoted exclusively to the priests and Levites. It is also true to a lesser degree for such passages as 2 Chronicles 5:11–13; 8:14; 29, and 31:11–19. The nature of the difficulty becomes apparent in such passages as 1 Chronicles 15, where Obed-edom is named three times (vv 18, 21, 24) in at least two different positions, or in chapter 25, where three groups of Levites are headed by Asaph, Heman, and Jeduthun (as also in 1 Chronicles 16:41), while in 1 Chronicles 15:17, Asaph and Heman occur with Ethan. It is also clear in the explicit but limited involvement of the Levites in such passages as 2 Chronicles 5:4 and even 5:12–13 or 35:3 as contrasted with the elaborate detail of, for example, 1 Chronicles 15 and 2 Chronicles 23, or 29–31.

What is in question, then, is not the involvement of

1, 2 CHRONICLES

the priests or Levites in the Chronicler's work, but rather the degree of elaboration and detail associated with that involvement. By its very nature such elaboration is most difficult to detect, and different readers will arrive at contrary judgments.

Finally, however, (3) the subject of priests and Levites can be left aside without disruption of the Chronicler's message because their positions and activity are so closely bound up with that of the temple. The writer may well have been closely involved in the affairs of the priests and Levites—he may even himself have felt strongly about the relative importance of the two groups. (See, for example, 2 Chronicles 29:34.) Ultimately, however, it was not the position of priest or Levite, but that of the Jerusalem temple at which they served that was determinative for the writer's position.

The purpose of the temple

Finally, we must ask why the temple was of such importance to the Chronicler, and why it is for our study. The temple was for Chronicles, like Kings, the place where God had caused his name to dwell, to which prayers might be directed with the assurance they would be heard. However, Chronicles found this understanding inadequate in another sense, and in two cases (2 Chr 2:4; 7:12) has described the temple also as a place of sacrifice. The temple is God's house, but he is not confined there (2 Chr 6:18 = 1 Kgs 8:27, stated earlier in 2:6, a section unique to Chronicles). Notice also that while 1 Chronicles 28:2 speaks of the temple as a house of rest "for the ark of the covenant," 1 Chronicles 23:25—which is perhaps late—speaks of God's dwelling in Jerusalem forever. But the occasional inclusion of an ancient bit of poetry such as that found in 2 Chronicles 6:1–2 (cf. 1 Kgs 8:12–13) or 2 Chronicles 6:41 (cf. Ps 132:8–9), where the temple is viewed as the resting place of both the ark *and* Yahweh, suggests that in the writer's mind the two concepts were not always clearly distinguished.

For the writer, it is certainly fair to say, participation in the observances of the Jerusalem temple was most closely identified with faith in and seeking Yahweh. "Yahweh is our God," Abijah could proclaim before Jeroboam, because Judah had not forsaken the Lord. She had legitimate priests and Levites, and the temple services were being observed as ordained (2 Chr 13:10–12). Hezekiah's invitation to the north to return to Jerusalem to worship, which would have been delivered shortly after the fall of the north to the Assyrians in 721 B.C., is full of significance:

> Do not be stiff-necked now as your fathers were, but yield yourselves to Yahweh, *and come to his sanctuary,* which he has sanctified for ever, and serve Yahweh your God, that his fierce anger may turn away from you. (2 Chr 30:8)

Indeed, Judah's own unfaithfulness will be symbolized by the destruction of the temple which they had forsaken (2 Chr 36:19).

In his own age, whenever it may have been, the author's faith must have looked upon the restoration of the proper temple services as the first priority in the reestablishment of the nation. The special appeals to the north throughout the book suggest a writing from the time when such an appeal would have been particularly appropriate, but such occasions in a long and contested history would not have been uncommon. A call for faithful dedication to the temple service would be equally appropriate if the author wrote sometime before the destruction of Jerusalem in 586 B.C., at the end of the Exile in 538 B.C.—as the current ending of the book would suggest (2 Chr 36:22–23)—at the time of the dedication of the second temple (Ezra 6:15–22), or at a later period when the temple had been rebuilt but was not being given the faithful devotion it deserved and required. For this last period, see the book of Malachi, usually dated in the first half of the fifth century B.C., or Ezra and Nehemiah, at the end of the same century. Amid the doubts, disappointments, and despair of whatever age, the message of the writer rang out: "O people of Israel, return to Yahweh, the God of Abraham, Isaac, and Israel. . . . Do not be like your fathers and your brothers, who were faithless . . ." (2 Chr 30:6–7). And for Chronicles, that meant returning to the temple at Jerusalem.

Readers in our day are apt to be somewhat put off by such a concentration upon a building, no matter how exceptional, and upon institutions which are at best reminders of and pointers to a greater reality. Without denying the close and positive relationship between the physical and the spiritual, we are apt to be uncomfortable in the face of an appeal which identifies symbol and reality so closely, and equates faith in God and presence at a building so nearly. Perhaps this is an equation which we are simply unable or unwilling to grasp.

In the New Testament we will find such of the faithful as Mary the mother of Jesus, Zechariah and Elizabeth, Anna and Simeon, in the temple. Joseph and Mary take the young Jesus to the temple, and the only event in Jesus' life recorded in the Gospels between his infancy and the beginning of his ministry is a visit to the temple with his family at the age of twelve (Luke 2:42) for the Passover. Despite the opposition he incurred, Jesus regularly frequented the temple and the synagogues. His disciples later would do the same, normally withdrawing only when required to do so. The temple and synagogue were important and vital institutions in the early days of the church.

Nevertheless, the symbolic and temporary nature of even these sanctified precincts is clearly recognized, as they were also in the Hebrew Scriptures. To the woman in Samaria who asks Jesus about the locale of the approved place of worship, Jesus responds:

"Woman, believe me, the hour is coming when neither on this mountain nor in Jerusalem will you worship the Father. . . . But the hour is coming, and now is, when the true worshipers will worship the Father in spirit and truth, for such the Father seeks to worship him. God is spirit, and those who worship him must worship in spirit and truth." (John 4:21, 23–24 RSV)

Moreover the same Gospel of John actually views Jesus himself as the replacement for the temple. When pressured by the Jews to give a sign to justify his cleansing of the temple, which story John symbolically places at the beginning of Jesus' ministry, Jesus replies: "Destroy this temple, and in three days I will raise it up" (John 2:19 RSV). The Jews naturally interpret the reference to be to the physical temple, which they note had been under construction for no less than forty-six years. But John states, "he spoke of the temple of his body" (2:21). When that is present of which the physical temple is only the symbol, the symbol fades into insignificance.

A parallel thought occurs in the Revelation of John, which concludes with the vision of a new heaven and a new earth, and the holy city Jerusalem coming down out of heaven from God. But the writer exclaims:

"And I saw no temple in the city, for its temple is the Lord God the Almighty and the Lamb. And the city has no need of sun or moon to shine upon it, for the glory of God is its light, and its lamp is the Lamb." (Rev 21:22–23 RSV)

When God himself dwells with his people, there will no longer be need of such material symbols of his presence as the temple. Until that time, however, our relationship with the spiritual is mediated through the physical. The incarnation of Jesus is the strongest testimony to that fact, and the sacraments of the church are aptly referred to as "the means of grace." With all their failings, religious symbols continue to speak to us in terms we can understand of the God who does not dwell in houses made with hands, but who nevertheless condescends to tabernacle with his people (John 1:14).

3

THE KINGDOM OF GOD

Then Abijah stood up on Mount Zemaraim which is in the hill country of Ephraim, and said, "Hear me, O Jeroboam and all Israel! Ought you not to know that Yahweh, the God of Israel, gave the kingship over Israel for ever to David and his sons by a covenant of salt? . . . and now you think to withstand the kingdom of Yahweh in the hand of the sons of David. . . . (2 Chr 13:4, 8 RSV)

The kingdom of God is, as the passage above indicates, "the kingdom of Yahweh in the hand of the sons of David." Yahweh himself had rejected Saul's house in favor of David's. "Saul died for his unfaithfulness," writes the Chronicler. "Therefore Yahweh slew him and turned the kingdom over to David the son of Jesse" (1 Chr 10:13–14).

In DH it may be true that prior to Solomon's death the identity of the specific Davidic king who would sit upon the throne was questionable, and that after Solomon's defection the ten northern tribes remained a kingdom (1 Kgs

11:34–35) and Jeroboam was offered what might likewise be called an "eternal dynasty" (1 Kgs 11:38), but this is not the case in Chronicles. While God's People might dwell in Israel or Judah (see pp. 49–56), God's kingdom is associated solely with the south, where the kings of David's line rule. And in every case, which of David's descendants will occupy the throne is clearly stated. In understanding the significance of the Davidic dynasty in Chronicles, and its relationship to the temple, the presentation of the reigns of David and Solomon is crucial.

David

The significance of David for Chronicles is well-known and commonly recognized. David figures prominently in 1 Chronicles 11–29, dominating no less than nineteen of the two books' sixty-five chapters. And they are important chapters. It is commonly recognized that the subjects of the temple, the priesthood, and the Levites lie at or near the center of Chronicles, and these three topics also figure prominently in these "David" chapters. Nor has the different picture which Chronicles paints of David over against that of Samuel-Kings escaped notice. No less a figure than Julius Wellhausen commented:

> See what Chronicles has made out of David: The founder of the kingdom has become the founder of the temple and the public worship, the king and hero at the head of his companions in arms has become the singer and master of ceremonies at the head of a swarm of priests and Levites, his clearly cut figure has become a feeble holy picture, seen through a cloud of incense.[1]

Gerhard von Rad's important monograph[2] pointed to the significance of David throughout Chronicles, and that significance has continued to be affirmed by most scholars. And yet the picture is not as clear as it might be. Some of the space devoted to David in Chronicles might be attributed to the fact that in Samuel-Kings also David is a dominant figure. The story of his reign fills all of the book of 2 Samuel, or twenty-four chapters. Moreover, David actually makes his appearance in 1 Samuel 16, and is actually of equal importance to Saul—if not surpassing Saul—in the remaining fifteen chapters of that book. Viewed in that light, the proportion of space devoted to David in Chronicles is considerably less.

It is not always proper to judge the importance of a person, theme, or topic by the number of words or chapters devoted to it, of course, although it is certainly not a bad measure to begin with in biblical studies. Consider, for example, that in the Old Testament Israel arrives at Sinai, the site of God's covenant with his people and the giving of the Law, in Exodus 19, and does not leave until Numbers 10:11. Or consider that, in the New Testament, each of the Gospel writers devotes a disproportionately large space to the Passion History, a single week in the life of Jesus.

But to be weighed also is the fact that, in his considerably briefer work, the Chronicler devotes a minimum of nine chapters to Solomon, compared with eleven in the Deuteronomistic History (1 Kgs 1–11), and that 1 Chronicles 22, 28, and 29 have Solomon as much as David as their subject. Indeed, if the temple lies at the heart of Chronicles, these chapters must be attributed first of all to Solomon, since in them he is designated as the divinely chosen instrument to build the temple, while David is explicitly disqualified from that activity due to the many wars which he conducted.

To see more carefully Chronicles' attitude toward David and Solomon, it is necessary to review the portrait of these two kings as the writer found it before him in Samuel-Kings. We can focus our attention upon (1) the manner in which the rise of the king to power is depicted, including the response of the people to his kingship; (2) his position in the dynastic lineage; (3) his relationship to the cult (public worship); (4) the role attributed to him in the division of the kingdom; and (5) the general evaluation given him by the respective writer. Finally, we will include other materials which point to the significant role Solomon occupied for the writer of Chronicles.

David in the Deuteronomistic History

In the Deuteronomistic History (DH), David is anointed king while Saul still occupies the throne, and "the Spirit of Yahweh came mightily upon David from that day forward" (1 Sam 16:13 RSV). While the writer presents the difficulties which David experienced in his rise to power vividly and in detail, the support which David receives from the people is presented as ever-increasing (1 Sam 16:6–8, 16; 2 Sam 3:36). And his ultimate success in the achievement of his God-given role seems assured from the time of his anointing by the prophet Samuel at Yahweh's command (1 Sam 16:12).

Yahweh's presence with David is repeatedly affirmed (1 Sam 18:14, 28; 2 Sam 5:10; 7:3). And even prior to the Dynastic Oracle of 2 Samuel 7, friends and foe alike repeatedly voice the conviction that Yahweh has chosen David to rule over his kingdom (1 Sam 20:15; 23:17; 24:20; 25:28; 26:25; 28:17; 2 Sam 3:9–10, 18).

Although Samuel records numerous events picturing David as deceptive, no judgment is pronounced upon these acts. The writer instead emphasizes David's constant loyalty to Saul as Yahweh's anointed (1 Sam 22:14; 24:6, 17; 2 Sam 1:16), contrasting David's guilelessness with Saul's treachery and deceit (e.g., 1 Sam 18:12–16, 28–29; 2 Sam 3:1).

After Saul's death, David is first anointed ruler over Judah (alone) at Hebron, where he rules seven and one-half years.

After an extended period of conflict with Saul's house, Israel too makes a covenant with David, and David rules over "all Israel," i.e., a united Judah and Israel, for thirty-three years from Jerusalem (2 Sam 5:3-5).

Although David is not permitted to build the temple, the Dynastic Oracle of 2 Samuel 7 promises that a nameless seed "who will come forth from his loins" will both have his kingdom established and will build the temple (vv 12-13), so that even if a king commits iniquity Yahweh will not withdraw his steadfast love (Heb. ḥesed) from him (vv 14-15). References to David's position as the founder of the dynasty and the recipient of the promise are frequent throughout Kings.

Concerning David's relationship to Israel's worship, Samuel reports that David had the ark brought to Jerusalem immediately upon his conquest of the city (2 Sam 6) and that he pitched a tent for it. No details are given concerning this tent, although one might assume that, if not in violation of tradition, it would have been quite elaborate. There is no mention of the involvement of cultic personnel, nor is there any indication that David made any provisions for construction of the temple, although the later statement that Solomon "brought in the things which David his father had dedicated—the silver, the gold, the vessels—and stored them in the treasuries of the house of Yahweh" (1 Kgs 7:51) could possibly be so interpreted.

At only two points does DH record God's displeasure with David. Following David's adultery with Bathsheba and his murder of her husband Uriah, Yahweh sends the prophet Nathan to condemn David (2 Sam 12:1). While David's sins are forgiven upon his confession, much of the remainder of the Court History seems to place David under the curse announced by 2 Sam 12:10-11: "Now therefore the sword shall never depart from your house . . . . I will raise up evil against you out of your own house . . ." (RSV). David's

action in conducting a census of Israel is similarly condemned, but the acceptance of his sacrifice again points to
his forgiveness (2 Sam 24). On his deathbed David, at the
urging of Bathsheba and Nathan, appoints Solomon as his
successor, so that the perpetuation of the dynastic line
through him continues to be acknowledged (1 Kgs 1).

Although Kings does not record a customary closing evaluation of David, it is clear that the author considers David
the primary example of the good king, in comparison with
whom other kings are judged. Numerous kings are judged in
accordance with whether they "walked in the way of David"
or "did right like David" (1 Kgs 3:3, 14; 9:4; 11:4, 6, 33, 38;
2 Kgs 14:3; 16:2; 18:3; 22:2). In one case David's murder of
Uriah is included in such a formula as the sole example
of David's misconduct (1 Kgs 15:5).

David in Chronicles

Most of the material picturing David as the scheming or
ruthless leader of an outlaw band or as a man who could
control neither his own passions nor his family is absent from
Chronicles. However, the reason lies perhaps not so much in
the writer's desire to aggrandize David as in the desire to
sharpen his focus upon the temple, and in the related desire
to demonstrate the support of "all Israel" for every work of
David (and Solomon) in that regard.

For details of the Chronicler's presentation of these two
aspects of David's career, see the summary provided under
"All Israel," pages 47-50. Here it may be stated simply that
any and every sign of opposition to David's rule has been
omitted, that David's kingship is recognized as in accord
with Yahweh's word and supported by "all Israel," and that,
after his anointing, David proceeds immediately to the cap-
ture of Jerusalem (1 Chr 11:4-9), destined to become the
home of the ark and the temple. This concern is central in

chapters 13–16, which conclude with the ark in Jerusalem, and in chapter 21, which culminates with David's choice of the threshing floor of Ornan as the site for the temple.

In 1 Chronicles 17 the dynastic oracle of 2 Samuel 7 is reproduced with minor variations. David's affair with Bathsheba and the murder of Uriah are omitted. Our survey of the temple materials in 1 Chronicles 22, 28–29 has shown how David undertook preparations for both building materials and workmen for the task ahead, entrusted to Solomon the task of erecting the temple, and provided Solomon with inspired plans to guide the work. David himself, however, is forbidden to build the temple because he "had shed much blood, and waged great wars" (2 Chr 22:8). (Compare also 1 Chronicles 17:4, where David's disqualification to build the temple is expressed more strongly than in 2 Samuel 7.)

The book of 2 Chronicles contains some thirty-five references to David without parallel in Kings. By far the most sizable group of these, apart from passages that speak only in general terms of David as the father of Solomon, has to do with David's relationship to cultic matters. Some of these have to do with building operations per se; in particular, 2 Chronicles 3:1 relates carefully how Solomon began to build the temple "in Jerusalem, on Mount Moriah, where Yahweh had appeared to David his father, at the place that David had appointed, on the threshing floor of Ornan the Jebusite" (RSV).

All in all, however, it appears that Chronicles has given a minimum of attention to David's role in the building of the temple. The focus is rather, as we shall see, upon Solomon, who conducts a census like David, secures timber and craftsmen like David, and begins construction of the temple at the place sanctioned by divine approval and appointed by David. In drawing this parallel between David and Solomon, however, the Chronicler does not disparage the work of

Solomon, but rather presents it as a part of a unified effort culminating in the completed temple.

Two related but different concerns are apparent in the remainder of the references dealing with David and the cult. The first of these has to do with David's relation to the music of the temple service. This is a new emphasis, since 1 Chronicles had spoken only of the personnel in charge of the music. But 2 Chronicles 7:6 speaks of the Levites who stood at their posts with instruments of music which David himself had made. A similar reference occurs in 2 Chronicles 29:26–27.[3]

Yet another kind of reference occurs in 2 Chronicles 29:30, where Hezekiah commands the Levites to sing praises with the *words* of David and Asaph the seer. Such an association of David with the lyrics of temple song is otherwise unknown in Chronicles, although the traditions of David's expertise in this area are well-known in other parts of the Old Testament (cf. 2 Sam 1:17–27; 23:1–2, and the psalm titles). While David was connected with Gad and Nathan in the previous passage, he is here associated with Asaph, who is called a seer.

Closely related to these passages, and at times intertwined with them, are others referring to David's organization of the priests and Levites. This concern was also found in 1 Chronicles, although it is difficult to determine which passages are original with the Chronicler.

The same difficulty is to be found in 2 Chronicles, where there is no agreement upon the authenticity of such passages as 8:14, 23:18, 29:25–30, and 35:4 and 15. However, there appears to be little reason to doubt the statements of 2 Chronicles 29:25–30 that the Levites connected with the temple music traced their office back through David and his prophets. If any of the other passages are from the hand of the Chronicler, the entire Levitical organization, without respect to individual function, may also be traced back to

David, although it was Solomon (2 Chr 8:14) who implemented those plans. That such was the case seems probable in view of 1 Chronicles 16:4. Of special note is the one case in which David and Solomon are coupled with regard to their directive for the Levites:

And he [Josiah] said to the Levites who taught all Israel and who were holy to Yahweh: "Put the holy ark in the house which Solomon the son of David, king of Israel, built; you need no longer carry it upon your shoulders. Now serve Yahweh your God and his people Israel. Prepare yourselves according to your fathers' houses by your divisions, following the directions of David king of Israel and the directions of Solomon his son. (2 Chr 35:3-4 RSV)

In Chronicles, as in DH, David is regarded as the founder of the dynasty. Abijah's famous speech reminds Jeroboam that "Yahweh has given the kingship forever to *David and his sons* by a covenant of salt" (2 Chr 13:5). In keeping with this dynastic emphasis, Chronicles has added as the conclusion of Solomon's dedicatory prayer in 2 Chronicles 6:41-42 a quotation from Psalms 132:8-9, which refers not only to the arrival of the ark in the temple but also to Yahweh's steadfast love (Heb. *ḥesed*) for David. All in all, however, there appears to be little change in the position accorded to the dynasty by Chronicles.

In Chronicles as in Samuel-Kings, David remains the exemplary king in comparison with whom others are judged. However, this occurs far less frequently in Chronicles than in Kings. In only four cases has the Chronicler taken over from DH a direct or implied statement of evaluation which mentions David (2 Chr 7:17; 28:1; 29:2; 34:2). In only one case has he added such an evaluation, noting that at the time of Rehoboam Judah walked for three years "in the way of

David and Solomon" (2 Chr 11:17), a phrase which parallels David and Solomon in a way quite inconceivable in the earlier history.

We may then summarize by noting that Chronicles has probably idealized David's rise to power to some degree, omitting all references to opposition to his reign and stressing the unanimous support of all Israel for that kingship. The great bulk of the Court History of David (2 Sam 9– 1 Kgs 2) has been omitted, including David's affair with Bathsheba and the murder of Uriah, although the reason for this is more open to question. The Chronicler has viewed David as the originator of the musical instruments of the cult, a contributor to the lyrics of some of the chants, and the one responsible for those Levitical groups concerned with music in the temple.

It is probable that the Chronicler has also viewed David as responsible for the remaining Levitical divisions, although the precise nature of his activity here is more difficult to evaluate. Chronicles has also stressed David's preparations for the building of the temple, and has him decree the building site, arrange for workmen and materials, and announce Solomon as the actual builder. On the other hand, we find no discernible attempt to emphasize David as the founder of the dynasty, and the use of David as a standard by which other kings are judged is minimized. The significance of this observation will become more apparent in studying the Chronicler's portrait of Solomon.

Solomon in the Deuteronomistic History

Though it seems to have been the understanding of DH that Solomon was the divinely chosen successor of David (2 Sam 12:24; 1 Kgs 5:3–5 [Heb. vv 15–17]), the author has not permitted this viewpoint to dominate his narrative of Solomon's accession to the throne. This is apparent above all from the inclusion in his work of the so-called Court History of David which relates in detail the strife among David's sons as to which will succeed him. It was only in response to Adonijah's power play that Solomon—supported by Bathsheba his mother, Nathan the prophet, Zadok the priest, and not least by Benaiah and David's army (1 Kgs 1:8)— emerged as the new king of Israel. Solomon then proceeded to secure his throne by arranging for the deaths of Adonijah and Joab, the general who had supported Adonijah, and by banishing Abiathar the priest. With all opposition effectively silenced, DH remarks pithily: "The kingdom was established in the hand of Solomon" (1 Kgs 2:46).

DH divides Solomon's reign into two distinct periods. The first of these extends from the beginning of his reign to the erection of the idolatrous high places, and views Solomon as an obedient king whose reign was characterized by the divine blessings of wisdom, prosperity, and peace. The erection of the temple occupies the center of Solomon's reign, and his dedicatory prayer points to that event as the climax of God's promises to Israel (1 Kgs 8:56). DH concludes this period of blessing with the account of the visit of the queen of Sheba and a summary of Solomon's wealth (1 Kgs 10).

The second period of Solomon's reign, however, sees Solomon as an apostate king who disobeyed Yahweh's command by marrying foreign wives, who erected high places for their gods and joined them in their idolatry. Solomon's frequenting of the high places *prior* to the building of the temple seems to have been largely condoned by DH, but the same surely cannot be said of the report in 1 Kings 11. There Solomon's marriage to foreign wives is explicitly condemned as a violation of God's command (v 2). It is twice stated that Solomon's heart was not completely true to Yahweh (vv 4, 6), and the high places he built are clearly considered idolatrous. It is commonly acknowledged that the strictures against kingship in Deuteronomy 17:16-17 refer in particular to Solomon (see 1 Kings 10:23-29), so that Solomon becomes in effect the parade example of the evils of kingship.

As a result, Yahweh becomes angry with Solomon (1 Kgs 11:9), and the division of the kingdom announced in verses 11-13 is the direct punishment for Solomon's sin. The account then proceeds immediately to speak of the "adversaries" (Heb. śāṭān, vv 14, 23, 25) whom God raised up against Solomon, marking the reversal of the conditions reported in 1 Kings 5:4 (Heb. 5:18), when there was "rest on every side" and there was "neither adversary (śāṭān) nor misfortune," so that Solomon could undertake the construction of the temple. Jeroboam's rebellion is given divine sanction by the prophet Ahijah (1 Kgs 11:31-39), the narrative of which is introduced with the words, "This was the reason why he [Jeroboam] lifted up his hand against the king" (v 27), followed again by a detailed reporting of Solomon's responsibility (v 33). Shemaiah's oracle preventing Rehoboam's attempt to regain the north gives additional force to the divine decree (1 Kgs 12:24).

The customary notice concerning Solomon's death is recorded in 1 Kings 11:41-43, and nothing favorable is reported concerning him in the remainder of the work. The writer never alters his view of Solomon as apostate until his death, as the one responsible for the high places to which the writer was so opposed, and as the sole cause for the disruption of the united kingdom. On the contrary, attention is specifically called to the fact that Josiah, whose reforming activity is the second high point within DH, broke down the high places Solomon had built, at last reversing the idolatrous practices begun by Solomon (2 Kgs 23:13-14).

Solomon in Chronicles

The picture of Solomon found in Chronicles stands in sharp contrast to that of DH. For the Chronicler, Solomon is, like David, king by divine choice, greeted with the unanimous support of all Israel and dedicated wholeheartedly to the cult. Like David, he too ends his long reign, as he had begun it, in peace and prosperity. But Solomon surpasses David in two ways. First, he is the divinely chosen temple builder. Secondly, in keeping with the added significance accorded Solomon as temple builder, Chronicles presents Solomon even more consistently as one who, from first to last, was completely faithful to Yahweh.

The manner in which Chronicles has restricted this presentation of Solomon to these concerns and the consistency with which the writer has pursued them can be fully appreciated only by an exhaustive comparison of DH and Chronicles. Here we can sketch only a few of the more striking details.

1. *Chronicles presents Solomon, like David, as king by divine choice.* The wording of the dynastic promise in 1 Chronicles 17:11 ("I will raise up your offspring after you, *one of your own sons* . . .", italics added) is perhaps only slightly more explicit than 2 Samuel 7:12-13, but the manner in which Chronicles has worked even the *name* Solomon into his statement of the promise in 1 Chronicles 22 is decisive:

"Behold a son shall be born to you; he shall be a man of rest (*'îš mᵉnûḥāh*). I will give him rest from all his enemies round about; *for his name will be Solomon* (*šᵉlōmōh*), and I will give peace and quiet (*šālôm wᵉšeqet*) to Israel in his days. He shall build a house for my name. He will be my son, and I will be his father, and I will establish the throne of his kingdom over Israel forever." (vv 9-10)

What was left open in the Dynastic Oracle is here made explicit: Solomon is the king divinely chosen by Yahweh to sit upon his throne. In David's second speech, the name

"Solomon" is similarly inserted: "It is Solomon your son who shall build my house and my courts, for I have chosen (Heb. *bāḥartî*, see page 11) him to be my son, and I will be his father" (1 Chr 28:6 RSV).

2. Secondly, *Chronicles presents all Israel as unanimous in her support of Solomon*. The competition and opposition to Solomon's kingship found in the early chapters of 1 Kings vanish in the face of the unanimous support of all Israel:

> And they made Solomon the son of David king the second time, and they anointed him as prince for the Lord, and Zadok as priest. Then Solomon sat on the throne of Yahweh as king instead of David his father; and he prospered, and *all Israel obeyed him. All the leaders and the mighty men, and also all the sons of King David, pledged their allegiance to King Solomon.* And the Lord gave Solomon great repute in the sight of all Israel. . . . (1 Chr 29:22b–25a)

Here, it should be noted, even David's other sons are among Solomon's supporters.

3. But, above all, *Chronicles presents Solomon as a king who—again like David his father—was a dedicated and zealous patron of the cult, and, more specifically, of the Jerusalem temple and its functionaries.* The writer, again, found the material for such a position at hand. The construction of the temple was for DH also the chief event of Solomon's life, totally occupying three lengthy chapters of his account of Solomon's reign (1 Kgs 6–8). Chronicles has, however, not simply reproduced the material of DH. Bypassing the material of 1 Kings 3–4, the writer has moved almost immediately to express Solomon's interest in the temple. The totality of 2 Chronicles 2–8 is devoted exclusively to that subject, introduced already in 2:1 (1:18, Heb.): "Solomon purposed to

build a temple for the name of Yahweh and a royal palace for himself" (RSV).

However, Chronicles' interest in Solomon's cultic concerns is evident in ways other than the sheer bulk of the material devoted to the subject. He has shown his interest in Solomon and the temple to be a lively one by the different way in which he has used his source material as well as by his structured and sympathetic treatment of the entire pericope.

In other portions of Chronicles the writer has confined himself largely to the deletion of some materials and the addition of others, with some minor alterations and comments. But Chronicles' account of Solomon, while dependent upon DH to a degree in almost every case, has amounted to almost a rewriting of the entire pericope.

We must limit our comments to a few examples.

Chronicles begins the narrative of Solomon's reign with the sacrifices at Gibeon (2 Chr 1:1-6), as had 1 Kings 3:1-4. But for Chronicles this is not a heterodox religious pilgrimage to a high place, but an orthodox procession of all Israel, led by its king, to a legitimate site of worship, since Moses' tent of meeting and the bronze altar are also there.

The materials of 2 Chronicles 2 provide a second example. After the initial statement of the theme (v 1), Solomon gathers laborers for the task and arranges with Huram of Tyre for the necessary materials. But the Chronicler has used Solomon's correspondence with Huram not only to request timber, as did DH (1 Kgs 5:3-6, Heb. 17-20). Through rewriting Solomon's message, he also includes what amounts to a confession of faith for Solomon and a significant statement of the purpose of the temple as a place of sacrifice (v 6). Solomon's request for a craftsman to direct the more delicate work— which stood quite alone in 1 Kings 7:13-14—is made part of Solomon's original request. Huram's reply is similarly altered.

Explicit statements added by the Chronicler assure us that the structure of the entire unit has been thoughtfully considered. The temple pericope (chs 2–8) is clearly delineated by remarks both at the beginning ("Now Solomon purposed to build a temple for the name of Yahweh . . . ," 2:1) and the end ("All the work of Solomon was completed, from the day of the foundation of the house of Yahweh until Solomon had completed the house of Yahweh," 2 Chr 8:16). Other stages within the temple narrative are similarly marked (cf. 3:1 and 5:1) and the conclusion added by Chronicles in 8:12–16, which understands the dedicatory festival as the institution of the regular temple services.

We may conclude, then, that as was the case with David, the Chronicler has ignored almost everything except cultic matters and Solomon's involvement in them. The essential similarity in the treatment of David and Solomon—both ruling by divine choice, both ruling with the unanimous consent of all Israel, both dedicated wholeheartedly to the temple and the cult—has commonly been overlooked or ignored by scholars intent on demonstrating the greater role attributed to David in the Chronicler's thought.

For the purpose of argumentation, two ways in which Chronicles' presentation of Solomon surpasses that of David may be pointed out. First, as has been noted repeatedly, it was in fact Solomon who built the temple. All of David's preparatory instructions and preparations notwithstanding, David is not permitted to erect this special house where God would cause his name to dwell, where Yahweh himself would rest among his people, this house of sacrifice where Yahweh would hear the prayers of his people. This greatest of all privileges was denied to David, the man of war, and given to Solomon, the man of peace.

Secondly, Chronicles has removed from the life of Solomon every taint of sin or fault—lengths to which he did not go in the depiction of David. Of the entire account of 1 Kings 11 nothing remains. There is here no story of Solomon's marriage to foreign women, or of high places (idolatrous or otherwise), and therefore the blame for the division of Israel and Judah does not rest upon him. Evidence from certain manuscripts of the Septuagint supports the conclusion that Chronicles was the first Old Testament writer to make Jeroboam responsible for this schism.[4]

Nevertheless, it would appear to be erroneous to pit David and Solomon against one another in the Chronicler's thought. It seems most likely that the writer wished to present the work of both as a single unit centering in the erection of the temple. With that in mind, we then can point to 1 Chronicles 22, 28, and 29 as the Chronicler's bridge unit for joining together the two parallel halves of this part of his work, i.e., the David History and the Solomon History.

Three specific passages can be pointed out where this paralleling of David and Solomon becomes explicit. Kings concludes the feast dedicating the temple by noting that Israel "went to their homes joyful and glad of heart for all the goodness that Yahweh had shown to David his servant and to Israel his people" (1 Kgs 8:66 RSV). Chronicles alters this passage to read "joyful and glad of heart for the goodness that Yahweh had shown to David and to Solomon and to Israel his people" (2 Chr 7:10, RSV, italics added).

Secondly, when Chronicles wishes to point to the faithfulness of Israel during the first part of Rehoboam's reign, the Chronicler states: ". . . for three years they [Israel] made Rehoboam the son of Solomon secure, for they walked for three years in the way of David and Solomon" (2 Chr 11:17, italics added). Such a statement would have been inconceivable for DH, who considered Solomon's idolatry the cause of the schism between north and south.

Finally, Josiah's words to the Levites at the conclusion of his reforms contain two examples where Solomon is placed beside or above David, one of these even with regard to Levitical arrangements:

And he [Josiah] said to the Levites who taught all Israel and who were holy to Yahweh, "Put the holy ark in the house which *Solomon the son of David*, king of Israel, built; you need no longer carry it upon your shoulders. Now serve Yahweh your God and his people Israel. Prepare yourselves according to your fathers' houses by your divisions, following the directions of *David, king of Israel, and the directions of Solomon, his son*. (2 Chr 35:3–4, italics added)

Post-Solomonic kings of Israel

Since Solomon was, according to Chronicles, blameless in his relationship to God, the fault leading to the rending of the kingdom under Rehoboam clearly did not lie with him, but with Rehoboam and the north. (Second Chronicles 10:15, which reproduces 1 Kings 12:15, must be judged an example of the author's retaining a statement from his original which he has otherwise chosen to dismiss.) Chronicles has, however, been able to reproduce the conclusion of the first part of that narrative from 1 Kings 12:19 without alteration: "So Israel has been in rebellion against the house of David to this day" (2 Chr 10:19).

This position is enunciated forcefully in 2 Chronicles 13, quoted at the head of this chapter. While it is possible here to read the emphases upon dynasty and temple as equal and supplementary (dynasty *and* temple), the emphasis, rather, lies upon the religious activities of the opposing dynasties. Jeroboam and his people have driven out the legitimate priests (v 9), while Abijah and his people have priests ministering to Yahweh who are legitimate Aaronites and Levites and who maintain the prescribed temple services (vv 10–11).

In this sense the north is "withstand[ing] the kingdom of Yahweh in the hands of the sons of David . . ." (v 8), and can be said to be fighting against Yahweh himself (v 12).

1, 2 CHRONICLES

The outcome of the ensuing battle is not in doubt: "Thus the men of Israel were subdued at that time, and the men of Judah prevailed, because they relied upon Yahweh, the God of their fathers" (2 Chr 13:18).

Chronicles and Messianism

In the remaining chapters of Chronicles, no emphasis upon the Davidic dynasty per se is apparent. The "kingdom of the Lord" is present, to be sure, and a king of David's line sits upon its earthly throne.

However, that kingdom is embodied in the "all Israel" who in faithful obedience to the Lord supports his worship at the temple in Jerusalem. The climax of this last part of the Chronicler's history is clearly reached with the reign of Hezekiah (2 Chr 29–32), but the focus of his kingship too is clearly to be found in the temple. He restores the service of the house of the Lord (29:35) and his invitation to the north is an invitation to return, not to his kingship, but to the sanctuary of the Lord (30:8).

Josiah's rather anticlimactic reign too is conspicuous because of the religious reforms already related in 1 Kings 22. These are, however, supplemented by additional reforms reaching into the north (2 Chr 34:6), with the establishment of the priestly and Levitical offices as directed by David and Solomon(!), and the celebration of a Passover, the likes of which had not been seen since the days of Samuel (2 Chr 35:4, 18). The final words of the book mention no Davidic hope, not even of the sort adumbrated in the final verses of DH in 2 Kings 25:27–29. It is instead the Persian king Cyrus to whom Yahweh is represented as speaking, and who gives decree that Yahweh's people return to Jerusalem to build him a house (2 Chr 36:22–23).

Some have nevertheless concluded that Chronicles does maintain a Messianic hope, based upon the significant position of the Davidic dynastic in such passages as 2 Chronicles 13:5, or upon the apparent fervor of such passages as 1 Chronicles 12:38–39 (Heb. vv 39–40), or the position of Zerubbabel in Ezra and Nehemiah (cf. Ezra 5:2). With the increasing doubt of the unity of Chronicles and Ezra-Nehemiah, it seems wiser to assume that Chronicles viewed the work of the Davidic dynasty as essentially completed with the construction of the temple, in which the hopes of the kingdom of God among Israel now lay.

Israel's hopes for the present lay in her relationship to the temple, which was the embodiment of God's kingdom, or rule, in her midst.

The kingdom of God in the New Testament

Among the most common phrases found in the New Testament are "the kingdom of God" and, in the wording preferred by Matthew, "the kingdom of heaven." The kingdom of God means, as one scholar put it, "all the trouble that God went to to establish his rule among people." The New Testament sets itself forth as being the record of the establishment of that rule.

This kingdom, it should be noted, is the kingdom of God in the hands of the son of David. Jesus is Israel's king, from the line of David, both David's son by the flesh and David's Lord by virtue of his divinity. That he commonly applies to himself the ambiguous title "Son of man" can mean, according to the Hebrew idiom, an ordinary man (cf. Ps 8:4; Ezek 34:2; 35:2; 36:1); in dependence upon the vision of Daniel 7:13, it can mean a heavenly figure. That he avoided the use of the word "king" is a realization that Jesus was not the kind of king commonly expected. Compare Jesus' conversation about kingship with Pilate in John 18:33–37.

Both Matthew and Mark summarize the message of Jesus as being Good News about the kingdom of God:

1, 2 CHRONICLES

Now after John was arrested, Jesus came into Galilee, preaching the gospel of God, and saying, "The time is fulfilled, and the kingdom of God is at hand; repent, and believe in the gospel." (Mark 1:14–15 RSV; cf. Matt 3:2; 4:17)

The same is true of Luke, who presents Jesus' initial activity after his temptation as a sermon delivered in the synagogue in Nazareth. This sermon quotes Isaiah 61:1–2 and concludes with Jesus' words: "'Today this scripture has been fulfilled in your hearing'" (Luke 4:21 RSV). That this is understood as the message of the kingdom of God is clear from words spoken to another audience shortly thereafter:

"I must preach the good news of the kingdom of God to the other cities also; for I was sent for this purpose." (Luke 4:43 RSV)

It would carry us too far afield in a work of this nature to consider the important questions of the specific nature of that kingdom and the degree to which various New Testament writers viewed that kingdom as already realized with Jesus' presence or as a kingdom to make its appearance at a later day—in particular, at the last great day of the Lord (cf. Luke 17:20–21; 19:11; Acts 1:3, 6). Nevertheless, it is again the book of Revelation which sounds the final and triumphant note in the biblical drama of the kingdom of God:

Alleluia: for the Lord God omnipotent reigneth. . . . The kingdoms of this world are become the kingdoms of our Lord, and of his Christ; and he shall reign for ever and ever. (Rev 19:6; 11:15 KJV)

With that hope, and for that victory, God's people in all ages have waited and trusted.

4

THE PEOPLE OF GOD: ALL ISRAEL

Now when all this was finished, all Israel who were present went out to the cities of Judah and broke in pieces the pillars and hewed down the Asherim and broke down the high places and the altars throughout all Judah and Benjamin, and in Ephraim and Manasseh, until they had destroyed them all. Then all the people of Israel returned to their cities. . . . (2 Chr 31:1, italics added)

Chronicles is concerned from first to last with the concept of Israel, the people of God. It is concerned with who belongs to this people, and what sorts of activities they are about.

The rise of David (1 Chronicles 10–12)

Chronicles goes to great lengths to show the participation of all Israel in David's rise to power and his coronation as Israel's king. Indeed, this appears to be the author's primary purpose in the drafting of chapters 10 through 12.

A tendency in this direction lay before the author in DH. There too David assembled "all Israel" to Hebron (2 Sam 5:1) and all Israel proceeded to Jerusalem to take the city (2 Sam 5:6; cf. 6:1-2). But Chronicles, as is its custom, has carried through this theme much more pervasively. The reason for the alteration found in 1 Chronicles 10:6 ("Thus Saul died . . . and his three sons and *all his house* died together"; cf. 1 Sam 30:6) is due to this tendency to include all of the nation in the acts of its kings. The same can be said of the omission of 2 Samuel 1-4 from Chronicles. For similar alterations compare 1 Chronicles 11:1 with 2 Samuel 5:6.

The remainder of chapters 11 and 12 brings together various lists of David's soldiers, including the tribal listings of 12:24-37 (Heb. 12:25-38). Here too the purpose is to show the support given David by all Israel. cf. 12:38-39 (Heb. vv 39-40):

> All these warriors, equipped for battle, came to Hebron with perfect heart to make David king over *all Israel*. And also *all the rest of Israel* was of one mind to make David king.

David and the ark (1 Chronicles 13-17)

The same theme is apparent also in the account of the transferral of the ark to Jerusalem (chs 13-17). Again the text, unique to Chronicles, points this out with almost humorous thoroughness:

> Then David consulted with the commanders of the thousands and hundreds, with *every leader*. David said to *all the assembly* of Israel: "If it seems good to you . . . let us send to *our brethren* who remain in *all the lands of Israel*, together with the priests and the Levites in the cities of their pasture lands, that they may

1, 2 CHRONICLES

gather to us, and let us bring back the ark of our God to us, because we did not seek it in the days of Saul." *All the assembly* said to do so, for the thing was right in the eyes of *all the people.* (1 Chr 13:1–4, italics added)

The narrative is then continued with words borrowed from 2 Samuel 6:1–11, but again with added emphasis upon the participation of all Israel in the proceedings: "So David assembled *all Israel* . . . and David and *all Israel* went up . . . and David and *all the Israelites* were celebrating with all their might . . ." (1 Chr 13:5–7, italics added; see also 1 Chronicles 15:3, 28).

All Israel and the temple

While chapters 17–21 are much more closely related to the writer's source (in 2 Samuel 7–11:1; 12:26, 30–31; 21:18–22; 24), the emphasis upon the unanimous participation of all Israel returns to the fore in 1 Chronicles 22 and 28–29 and in 2 Chronicles 1–9. In the former, David designates Solomon as the divinely chosen builder of the temple; the latter reports the events of Solomon's reign, including the construction and dedication of the temple.

All Israel's leaders are to help Solomon in his work (1 Chr 22:17, perhaps a later addition to the Chronicler's work). After revealing this to Solomon, David summons all the leaders of Israel to Jerusalem (1 Chr 28:1), and the position of the entire assembly is emphasized repeatedly (1 Chr 28:8, 21; 29:1, 6, 20). Sacrifices are offered for "all Israel" (29:21), and Solomon is obeyed by "all Israel" (29:23). Verse 24 is particularly pointed in its wording:

All the officers and mighty men, as well as all of King David's sons, pledged their submission to King Solomon. (1 Chr 29:24)

During Solomon's reign, too, the participation and support of all Israel is noted at particularly significant moments. Chronicles transforms Solomon's sacrifice at the idolatrous high place at Gibeon into a legitimate sacrifice before the tent of meeting, which was located there (1 Chr 16:39-40). Fittingly, all Israel participates with him (2 Chr 1:2-3).

Again, the participation of all Israel in bringing the ark up to the completed temple had already been mentioned by Kings (1 Kgs 8:1-3; 2 Chr 5:3-5). The same is true of the dedicatory feast for the temple (2 Chr 7:8; cf. 1 Kgs 8:65). In these same passages the broadest geographical extent of Israel is mentioned—from the entrance of Hamath in the north to the wadi of Egypt in the south.

After the death of Solomon and the division of the kingdom, the concept of "all Israel" admittedly changes. Like DH, the Chronicler has Rehoboam appear before "all Israel" at Shechem to be made king (2 Chr 10:1 = 1 Kgs 12:1). The Chronicler can use "Israel" and "all Israel" for the northern tribes (cf. 2 Chr 13:4, 5, 15, 18), in contrast to the southern tribes, which are variously designated as "Judah" (2 Chr 14:4, 7), "Judah and Benjamin" (2 Chr 15:2, 8-9; 31:1), and "Judah and Benjamin and the inhabitants of Jerusalem" (2 Chr 34:9). But the name "Israel" also applies to the south, or at least a portion of it (2 Chr 24:5-6). The use of such a qualifying phrase as "the people of Israel *who dwelt in* the cities of Judah" (2 Chr 10:17 = 1 Kgs 12:17) points to a narrower meaning of Israel as the faithful component among the people. And while the Chronicler admittedly concentrates upon the southern tribes, he does not forget that the entire land, including the north, is within the ideal limits of the holy land "from Beersheba to Dan" (2 Chr 30:5). True worshipers from both north and south will compose the true Israel (2 Chr 31:1; 35:17-18).

All Israel in 2 Chronicles 10–36

The writer's concern for all Israel in the post-Solomonic period shows itself primarily in two ways: (1) Various southern kings in this period are viewed as active in the north, both in military activities and in introducing religious reforms; and (2) the participation of Israelites from the north in the legitimate worship at Jerusalem is regularly noted.

Chapters 10–36 show a continuing concern for the problem raised by the apostasy of the north. This concern is portrayed on several different levels.

First, Chronicles reports that Abijah (13:19), Asa (15:8), and Jehoshaphat (17:2) all captured various northern cities and, in the last case, fortified them. While this fact alone could be used to support the writer's vindictiveness toward the north, this need not be the case. Immediately after the division of the kingdom, Chronicles records that priests, Levites, "and those who had set their hearts to seek Yahweh the God of Israel came . . . from all the tribes of Israel to Jerusalem to sacrifice to Yahweh" (11:16 RSV), thus strengthening the kingdom of Rehoboam. The significance of the terminology here is readily apparent, since the phrase "to seek Yahweh" is the Chronicler's way of describing faithful Yahwists. The statement that these people came *to Jerusalem*, and that they came *to sacrifice* to Yahweh, likewise reflects a characteristic emphasis of Chronicles.

After Asa's reforming activity in both north and south is mentioned (15:8), Chronicles also tells of a covenant made at Jerusalem which includes people from "Ephraim, Manasseh, and Simeon" who were at this time "sojourning" (Heb. *gērîm*) in the south. The language is again explicit: "for great numbers had deserted to him from Israel when they saw that Yahweh his God was with him"

(15:9). The twin themes of seeking Yahweh and sacrificing to him are again present in the description of the covenant (15:11, 13).

In addition to the fact that sizable numbers from the northern tribes recognized the legitimacy of the south's dynasty and cult and defected to the south, Chronicles frequently relates various types of religious reforms pursued by Judean kings. As mentioned, Asa removes idolatrous images from Judah and Benjamin, and also "from the cities which he had taken in the hill country of Ephraim . . ." (15:8). Hezekiah's religious zeal in bringing people back to Yahweh is noted as extending "from Beersheba to Dan" (30:5). All Israel was to come to Jerusalem to keep the Passover, and it noted that, while his messengers met with some scorn and ridicule in their journeys, "some men[1] from Asher, Manasseh, and Zebulun humbled themselves and came to Jerusalem" (30:11, WBC 15).

The favorable response to Hezekiah's invitation on the part of these northerners resulted in their participation in Hezekiah's delayed Passover, which is the high point of the Chronicles narrative of the post-Solomonic kings. While there is less emphasis upon the involvement of the north in Josiah's Passover, where the role of the Levites receives primary attention, the mention of "all Judah and Israel who were present, and the inhabitants of Jerusalem" (35:18) clearly includes the northern tribes and indicated that "all Israel" (v 17) should also be understood to include the north. This means that a contingent from the north was present for Asa's covenant ceremony (2 Chr 15) as well as for both of the major festivals celebrated by post-Solomonic kings, the Passovers of Hezekiah and Josiah.

It is also reported that these same three kings undertook reforming activities in the north. Asa destroyed the idols in both north and south (15:8). While 2 Kings 18:4 had noted

Hezekiah's reforming activity in the south, Chronicles ascribes to the Israel present for the Passover (which we have seen included a delegation from the north) the destruction of high places also in Ephraim and Manasseh (31:1). The account of Josiah's reform in 2 Kings 23:15-20 includes the destruction of high places in the north. And although it is rewritten by the Chronicler in a more general fashion, it retains its emphasis upon reforms both in the south and in "the cities of Manasseh, Ephraim, and Simeon, and as far as Naphtali" (2 Chr 34:6).

A scattering of other references pointing to an ongoing concern for the Israelites of the north also occurs. These include the double mention of the sacrifices offered for all Israel at Hezekiah's rededication of the temple (29:24), perhaps recalling the similar statement of 1 Chronicles 29:21.

Within his account of Josiah, the Chronicler has included two episodes dealing sympathetically with the north. While Kings says the money collected for the necessary temple repairs was deposited in a chest in the temple (2 Kgs 22:4), the Chronicler has not only rewritten that to reflect more favorably upon the priests and Levites, but describes the Levites as receiving the offering "from Manasseh and Ephraim and from all the remnant of Israel and from all Judah and Benjamin and from the inhabitants of Jerusalem" (2 Chr 34:9). The comprehensiveness of this passage suggests the degree of the writer's concern. In the story of the discovery of the scroll in Josiah's time, the Chronicles account significantly introduces the north as an object of Josiah's concern (34:21) whereas according to the basic text of 2 Kings 22:13, King Josiah makes inquiry only concerning the south. In none of these cases, it should be noted, does the Chronicler berate the north or its representatives, but they are apparently accepted as completely equal to the faithful of the south.

Apostasy in the north

Finally, our consideration of the "all Israel" theme should look at three passages in which the writer has dealt at greater length with the north's apostasy. Chronicles ascribes the primary responsibility for the dissolution of the united monarchy to Jeroboam, largely absolving Rehoboam and Judah from guilt. The Chronicler has inserted his views of the north's apostasy in a lengthy speech by Abijah where two objections are raised: (1) Yahweh has given the kingship over Israel to David and his sons forever (2 Chr 13:5, 8), and (2) the north has forsaken Yahweh in driving out the Aaronic priests and the Levites from their territories, while the south has retained the legitimate priesthood and cult. It is therefore clear that Israel has forsaken Yahweh, and that he is not with them. Judah's victory is assured "because they relied upon Yahweh" (2 Chr 13:18). A half-million of the enemy's troops are killed.

The second passage, which has been inserted into the reign of Ahaz, is very different in its focus. In keeping with his dogma of retribution (see chapter 6), the writer has stated that as a result of the wickedness of Ahaz, Judah was given into the hand of the king of Syria and some 120,000 Judeans fell before Pekah of Israel "because they had forsaken Yahweh" (2 Chr 28:5-7). Moreover, the writer also reports that 200,000 women and children were taken captive by Israel and brought as spoil to Samaria. But a prophet of Yahweh was there (!), who urged the north to return their captives. Both his message to the soldiers and the reactions of the soldiers and the people are exceptional. The prophet Oded condemns the north because, while Yahweh was angry with Judah and had handed its army over to Israel, Israel had overstepped its allotted task both in the severity of the attack (v 9) and in its plans to make slaves of the women and children, who are described as relatives (Heb. *mē'aḥēkem*, v 11). Israel is reminded at the same time of its own sins and of the additional wrath which the present plans will bring upon Israel (vv 10–11).

The response of the Samaritan princes is remarkable indeed. Reiterating their own guilt, they persuade the armed men to leave the captives with them (v 14). The princes themselves then took the captives, provided them with food, clothing, and transportation for the infirm, and returned them to Jericho, a city apparently in Israelite hands at that time but whence they could easily enter Judah. W. Rudolph has remarked concerning the character of these first "Good Samaritans," upon which the New Testament story in Luke 10 seems to be at least remotely dependent.[2]

This passage notes the existence of faithful prophets of Yahweh in the north—more explicitly in Samaria—as well as of people obedient to their message. Although it is true that the emphasis here is upon Israel for overextending Yahweh's punishment upon Judah, the sins and guilt of both Israel and Judah are acknowledged. But an equal emphasis falls upon the godly character of the Samaritans, who respond positively to the prophet's words and have compassion upon their relatives from Judah.

The third passage requiring special attention in a discussion of all Israel is 2 Chronicles 30:1–31:1, where the participation of all Israel in Hezekiah's Passover is a major component. We have mentioned Hezekiah's invitation to the northern tribes to come to Jerusalem for the Passover and indicated that there was a more positive response than that suggested by many translations of 2 Chronicles 30:11. Here we need to call attention to the contents of Hezekiah's invitation in verses 6–9.

While it would be easy to emphasize the guilt which the message attributes to the north, as a result of which Israel has been laid waste by Assyria, to do so would negate the major thrust of the passage, which is clearly a call to repentance. The remnant left by the Assyrians is urged to take heed to the negative example of their faithless fathers, to give themselves to Yahweh and to return to his sanctuary (v 8).

They are given at least three reasons why they should do this, the first two of which are stated in terms of results: that Yahweh's anger might turn from them (v 8) and that their exiled relatives might find mercy in the hands of their captors and return to Israel. But the third reason for Israel to repent is to be found in the nature of Yahweh himself: "For Yahweh your God is gracious and merciful, and will not turn away his face from you, if you return to him" (v 9). Yahweh's grace, therefore, is readily available to those of the north who repent and turn to him, although it is apparent that for the Chronicler this "repentance" included a recognition of and return to the Jerusalem temple.

In the account of the Passover which follows, the note of the north's involvement is never permitted to wane. Verse 18 seems to state that, in particular, the representatives of various northern tribes had not been permitted to prepare themselves properly for eating the Passover as prescribed. Yet Hezekiah's prayer for forgiveness would be equally relevant to the south. That prayer proclaims emphatically that "setting the heart to seek Yahweh" is more important than obedience to cultic laws. Chronicles is then careful to add the note of Yahweh's approval (v 20), "And Yahweh heard Hezekiah, and healed [forgave?] the people."

The inclusion of the north among the people of Israel present in Jerusalem (v 21) and with "all the assembly" (qōl haqqāhāl, vv 23, 25) may then be assumed. The latter verse mentions specifically both the "whole assembly that came in from Israel" and also sojourners, resident aliens (Heb. gērîm) who had come in from the land of Israel to participate in the fourteen-day feast. The emphasis in the preceding verses upon the involvement of all parts of Israel strongly suggests that the paralleling of the event with the days of Solomon in verse 26 may refer specifically to the participation of both north and south in the feast. This would be particularly significant at the time of Hezekiah, when the north had just fallen to the Assyrians and ceased to exist as an independent kingdom.

Such a reading of Chronicles takes on added significance now, when the definitive break between Jews and Samaritans is being dated much later than it was in earlier decades,[3] and when the unity of Chronicles and Ezra-Nehemiah is no longer taken for granted. Earlier scholars maintained that at least a major purpose of Chronicles-Ezra-Nehemiah was to voice its opposition to the north. This attitude was found primarily in Ezra-Nehemiah, whence it was exported to Chronicles as well. Viewed impartially, Chronicles instead maintains that faithful Yahwists in both north and south who recognized the unique position of the Jerusalem temple belonged to the true Israel, the people of God, and were invited and welcome to participate in its worship.[4]

Israel in the New Testament

The concept of Israel and the question of who "all Israel" consists of is not confined to the Old Testament. Just as the New Testament was concerned to show its relationship with "the God of the fathers" (see chapter 1), so it absorbs also the name and the concept of Israel.

One principle which the New Testament uses in detailing the life of Jesus is what has been called *recapitulation*. This means in brief that whatever happened to Israel in the Old Testament happens again to and in Jesus. When as an infant Jesus goes down to Egypt to escape Herod's wrath and then returns, Matthew quotes as a fulfillment the words of Hosea 11:1: "Out of Egypt I called my son" (RSV). Just as Israel of old, God's children, came up from Egypt, so does Jesus, the new Israel (Matt 2:15).

After his baptism, which the church has regularly related to the deliverance experienced in the Exodus, Jesus undergoes a forty-day temptation in the wilderness, corresponding to Israel's forty years (Matt 4:1-11). The phraseology of Mark, which speaks only of Jesus being with the wild beasts, and of angels ministering to him (1:13), is particularly suggestive here. Jesus undergoes all that befell Israel of old, but with this exception: He yielded to no temptation. He committed no sin. Luke even reports that at the Transfiguration Moses and Elijah, embodiments of the Old Testament's legal and prophetic traditions, appeared speaking with Jesus "and spoke of his departure [exodus], which he was to accomplish at Jerusalem" (Luke 9:30 RSV).

Jesus is the embodiment of Israel of old, the perfect Israel existing in a single person. It is in that connection also that the great Servant Songs of Isaiah (Isa 42:1-9; 49:1-6: 52:13-53:12; 61:1-4) are applied directly to Jesus in explanation of the servant role in which he appeared. The words spoken by the Father at Jesus' baptism, "'Thou art my beloved Son; with thee I am well pleased'" (Mark 1:11 RSV) are taken from both Psalm 2:7, a Messianic psalm, and from Isaiah 42:1. The Son of Man, Jesus would say, "'came not to be served but to serve, and to give his life as a ransom for many'" (Mark 10:45 RSV).

But just as Israel of old came to be restricted ultimately to Jesus, the one perfect Israelite, so from Jesus proceeds a *new* Israel. The fact that Jesus called twelve apostles to follow him, and that upon the death of Judas it was felt necessary to choose another to preserve the number *twelve* (Acts 1:15-26), recalls the twelve tribes which originally composed "all Israel" and which the Chronicler was insistent on maintaining. The church, the Body of Christ, was itself to be the new

1, 2 CHRONICLES

people of God, the New Israel. Those who share the faith of Abraham are the children of Abraham (Rom 4:16). The problem of the relationship between the old Israel, the Jews, and the New Israel is discussed openly and pointedly (Acts 15, Gal 2, and Rom 9–10).

5

THE WORD OF GOD

Yahweh, the God of their fathers, sent persistently to them by his messengers, because he had compassion on his people and on his dwelling place; but they kept mocking the messengers of God, despising his words, and scoffing at his prophets, till the wrath of Yahweh rose against his people, till there was no forgiveness. (2 Chr 36:15-16)

The God of Israel, the God of the fathers, is a God who reveals himself to his people. He does this through his Word, spoken of old through spokesmen like Moses and encapsulated in the Torah, conventionally translated "Law," and through the prophets of the past and present.

References to the Law are not rare in Chronicles. It is above all the "law of Yahweh" (cf. 1 Chr 16:14; 22:12; 2 Chr 12:1; 17:9; 19:8, and others). It is also the Law of Moses (2 Chr 23:18; 30:16), and the Law in "the book of Moses" (2 Chr 25:4). This law is sometimes referred to in particular circumstances, such as the descriptions of Levitical arrangements (2 Chr 23:18–21) and the temple tax (2 Chr 24:9). King Jehoshaphat sends princes and Levites throughout the land to teach "having the book of the law of Yahweh with them" (2 Chr 17:9). The book of the Law found by Josiah in the temple is named by the Chronicler "the book of the law of Yahweh given through Moses" (2 Chr 34:14).

Nevertheless, one gets the impression that the Law per se is not of paramount importance in Chronicles. God has spoken and continues to speak through his messengers, the prophets, though the form and content of their messages may differ, even radically, from age to age and from situation to situation.

So when Chronicles states that Saul died because he did not keep the word of Yahweh (1 Chr 10:13), it seems clear that it is the word of a prophet that is in view. In the same way, Israel anointed David as king over Israel, says 2 Samuel 5:3; and the Chronicler adds, "according to the word of the Lord by Samuel" (1 Chr 11:3). The Chronicler introduces his list of David's mighty men with the phrase:

These are the heads of David's mighty men who supported him strongly in his kingdom with all Israel to make him king according to Yahweh's word concerning Israel. (1 Chr 11:10)

God addresses David through the prophet Nathan (1 Chr 17:3 = 2 Sam 7:3, apparently negating Nathan's earlier advice, which should accordingly be understood as personal in nature) and through the seer Gad (1 Chr 21:9 = 2 Sam 24:11). David himself relates the directive that forbids the building of the temple to a direct word from the Lord not recorded elsewhere: "'You have shed much blood and have waged great wars; you shall not build a house to my name . . .'" (1 Chr 22:8; cf. 28:3, 6).

Words of other prophets recorded in Samuel–Kings, such

as Shemaiah (2 Chr 12:5, 7), Micaiah (2 Chr 18), and the prophetess Huldah (2 Chr 34:22 = 2 Kgs 22:14), are also passed on.

Further prophets named in other canonical writings are also referred to in Chronicles, though their words are not recorded. Jehoram is said to have received a letter from Elijah the prophet (2 Chr 21:12). Other events from the reigns of Uzziah and Hezekiah are said to have been recorded by the prophet Isaiah (2 Chr 26:22; 32:32), whose prayer for Hezekiah is also noted (2 Chr 32:20). Jeremiah is said to have uttered a lament upon Josiah's death (2 Chr 35:25) and to have been ignored by Judah's last king, Zedekiah (2 Chr 36:12).

More interesting and unusual, however, are instances in which the Chronicler portrays God as speaking through otherwise unknown prophets and by unexpected means. In 2 Chronicles one reads also the words of Azariah, son of Obed (15:1-7), Hanani the seer (16:7-9), and of Jehu the son of Hanani (19:1-3) who chronicled the life of Jehoshaphat (20:34).

Here too one finds references to the words of Eliezer the son of Dodavahu (2 Chr 20:37), and to Obed, a prophet of Yahweh who was active in the north in the reign of the wicked Ahaz and who brought about the work of the first "Good Samaritans" (2 Chr 28:8-15). Second Chronicles speaks also of a nameless "man of God" who prophesied during the reign of Amaziah (25:7-9), and of another similarly unknown prophet (25:15-16). All appear to give emphasis to typical emphases of the Chronicler as known from the framework of his books and through the mouths of such kings as David, Solomon, and Abijah: Yahweh is with his people when they are with him; if they forsake him, he will forsake them. Israel's call is to be faithful to the Lord, to avoid foreign alliances, to keep his Law, including the prescribed worship at the Jerusalem temple.

Chronicles, however, does not confine the word of Yahweh to prophets of the traditional stamp. The same Spirit of God which came upon Azariah (2 Chr 15:1-7) is also said to have motivated one of David's mighty men, Amasai, to have spoken a verse in praise of David (1 Chr 12:18), and to have done the same to a Levite of Asaph's line, Jahaziel, in the assembly of the house of Yahweh (2 Chr 20:5, 14-17). This is also true of Zechariah, the son of the priest Jehoiada (2 Chr 24:20-22), who was subsequently stoned to death in the temple courts by the command of King Joash (2 Chr 24:20-22). That Chronicles stood at the end of the canon in the time of Jesus seems assured by his reference in Matthew 23:35 to the murders of Abel and of Zechariah as the first and the last recorded in the Old Testament.

The Word of God, in brief, is becoming either more or less institutionalized, depending upon one's purview. Soldiers, like David's mighty man, and especially Levites, whom we would define as members of the temple choir, are increasingly being viewed as vehicles of the divine Word. And the Spirit who clothed such exceptional heroes as Gideon (Judg 6:34), Jephthah (Judg 11:29), and David (1 Sam 16:13) is now operative in the more ordinary affairs of everyday life, and in particular among the priests and minor clergy of the Jerusalem temple. Such an understanding will reach its acme in 1 Chronicles 22-26, often considered a later addition to the Chronicler's original work. In that five-chapter passage, the musical work of the three chief groups of Levites—Asaph, Heman, and Jeduthun—is routinely described as prophesying (1 Chr 25:1-4; see also 2 Chronicles 29:30; 35:15).

That is not to say that the discovery of God's Word and will is to be found only among the institutional clergy. Various kings, such as David, Solomon, and Josiah, seem to proceed in many of their activities with the understanding that their decisions are divinely guided. This is particularly true with reference to the arrangements of and for the Levites, where it appears that fundamental decisions are tied to the Mosaic Law, but ongoing regulations are the work of David, Solomon, and perhaps other kings (1 Chr 23:1-6; 2 Chr 8:12-16; 29:25-30; 35:1-6). David is in fact said to have received the plans for at least the basic temple structure "in a writing from the hand of Yahweh" (1 Chr 28:19). Apparently no further explanation seemed necessary to the writer.

Finally, one must be aware of a communication between God and at least some of his people which lay outside of all ordinary and institutional channels. Two times the Lord is said to have appeared to Solomon in a dream (2 Chr 1:7-13; 7:12-18). The Lord responds to the people's repentance with forgiveness (2 Chr 12:6-7). They pray, and the Lord answers (2 Chr 32:24). Hezekiah even prays for people who celebrate the Passover in uncleanness and not according to the prescriptions of the sanctuary. And Yahweh hears his prayer and forgives or "heals" (wayyirpāʾ) the people (2 Chr 30:20). This is true even of such a miscreant as Manasseh (2 Chr 33:12-14).

The Word of God, as one of the ancient prayers of the church puts it, is not to be bound, but is to be preached to the joy and edifying of God's people. Even Pharaoh Necho of Egypt can become the means through which Yahweh communicates his will to people. In the final analysis only the rejection of that Word, sent persistently by the Lord because of his compassion, results in God's wrath poured out without healing or forgiveness (Heb. marpēʾ), until the land enjoys its sabbaths and the Word is again heard (2 Chr 36:15-16, 21-22).

Again, significant New Testament developments in the doctrines of the Word of God might be mentioned. Chief among these is the designation of Jesus Christ as the Word (Greek logos) of God, through whom God has spoken his

The Word of God   65

final and definitive word. The writer of Hebrews connects directly with the Old Testament witness when he notes:

In many and various ways God spoke of old to our fathers by the prophets; but in these last days he has spoken to us by a Son, whom he appointed the heir of all things, through whom also he created the world. (Heb 1:1-2 RSV)

The Prologue of John draws both upon rabbinic sources and Greek philosophy. In the former, God's Word was one of those elements like the Law, wisdom, the Messiah, the glory of God, and the spirit of God which were considered preexistent. In the latter, Greek philosophy, the *logos* was, among other things, both an emanation from the divine and the divine reason which ordered all things. The Prologue announces:

In the beginning was the Word, and the Word was with God, and the Word was God. He was in the beginning with God; all things were made through him, and without him was not anything made that was made. (John 1:1-3 RSV)

It is John's further pronouncement that this preincarnate Word has become incarnate, or taken on human flesh, in Jesus, God's unique Son in whom we see the Father:

And the Word became flesh and dwelt among us, full of grace and truth; we have beheld his glory, the glory as of the only Son from the Father. . . . And from his fulness have we all received, grace upon grace. For the law was given through Moses; grace and truth came through Jesus Christ. No one has ever seen God; the only Son, who is in the bosom of the Father, he has made him known. (John 1:14, 16-18)

This language and theology is continued and expanded in the church. The Nicene Creed does not use the title "Word," but does refer to Jesus as "begotten of his Father before all worlds, God out of God, Light out of Light, true God out of true God, begotten, not made, being of one substance with the Father, by whom [i.e., Jesus, the Word] all things were made. . . ."

Thus with the fullness of God's revelation achieved in Christ, most Christians anticipate no further revelation; the final chapter of the Bible is usually read as a warning against those who would claim to have new revelations from God (Rev 22:18). God's powerful Word, incarnate in his Son Jesus, will continue to govern and preserve all things until his final appearing.

6

DIVINE RETRIBUTION

In those days Hezekiah became sick and was at the point of death, and he prayed to Yahweh; and he answered him and gave him a sign. But Hezekiah did not make return according to the benefit done to him, for his heart was proud. Therefore wrath came upon him and Judah and Jerusalem. But Hezekiah humbled himself for the pride of his heart, both he and the inhabitants of Jerusalem, so that the wrath of Yahweh did not come upon them in the days of Hezekiah. (2 Chr 32:24–26)

By retribution is meant a reward or punishment corresponding to a good or evil deed. In that connection, it is fair to say that in Chronicles a good deed, as represented in the actions of a faithful king or people, *always* results in blessing, and that an evil deed, as defined by the author, *always* results in bane.

The concept of retribution, like many significant elements in the Chronicler's theology, is introduced in a major speech of David to Solomon. It is reiterated in prophetic speeches throughout the work and serves as the governing and organizing principle in the presentation of the histories of the post-Solomonic kings.

This dogma is expressed most clearly in the Chronicler's recitation of the histories of the post-Solomonic kings. It is fair to say that retribution is *the* dominant principle influencing the manner in which the Chronicler has dealt with the history of the various kings as he found them in the books of Kings.

The principle of retribution is given first expression in David's second speech to Solomon: "If you seek him [the Lord], he will be found by you; but if you forsake him, he will reject you forever" (1 Chr 28:9). It is reiterated explicitly in almost identical words through various prophets whom the writer presents as appearing from time to time: "The Lord is with you, while you are with him. If you seek him, he will be found by you, but if you forsake him, he will forsake you" (2 Chr 15:2; cf. 2 Chronicles 12:5; 14:7, and 16:7).

In *every* case in which the work of the Deuteronomic Historian might be considered deficient in this regard, Chronicles in some manner adjusts his text to remedy that deficiency. This is seen already in the reign of Solomon's son Rehoboam. Kings has noted without further explanation that during the reign of Rehoboam Judah had been invaded by Shishak of Egypt (1 Kgs 14:25). Chronicles, however, provides a cause for this invasion corresponding to his doctrine of retribution: Judah has been unfaithful, has abandoned God, and has forsaken the Law of the Lord (2 Chr 12:1, 2, 5). The words of the prophet Shemaiah make the correspondence complete: "Thus says the Lord, 'You abandoned me, so I have abandoned you to the hand of Shishak'" (2 Chr 12:5).

The terminology here is very general—no specific action of Judah is referred to. What is important is often not the *details*, but the *principle* that is involved. In a similar but positive frame, we will read of kings who repent (2 Chr 12:12), who rely upon the Lord, and who seek the Lord. The account of Rehoboam is a model of Chronicles' historiography. Kings has reported Shishak's invasion as dating in Rehoboam's fifth year. Chronicles fleshes out its account by adding material to complement this schema. Since retribution in Chronicles is always immediate, the writer concludes that Judah's apostasy occurred in the fourth year, and that, correspondingly, Rehoboam enjoyed a three-year period of faithfulness (identified here as walking in the ways of David *and Solomon*, 2 Chr 11:17). Such obedience results in a prosperity expressed by three of the means which we shall see are regularly indications of God's blessings: building operations, military might, and large families (11:5-12, 18-21, 22-23). Shishak's invasion during the fifth year results in military defeat and subjugation. Concerning Rehoboam's repentance, see page 101.

Chronicles uses the brief reign of Abijah for a different purpose, silently reversing the position represented in Kings that Abijah was an evil king. Instead, the mention of his warfare with Jeroboam of the north provides the opportunity for a detailed speech summarizing the author's position: Judah has the legitimate king and the legitimate priesthood, while Israel is in rebellion against God. With that in mind, the outcome of the battle is never in doubt. Five hundred thousand Israelites are slain, "and the men of Judah prevailed, because they relied upon Yahweh" (2 Chr 13:18 RSV). Additional signs of the prosperity attending Abijah follow: Abijah captures three additional cities of Israel, grows in strength, and has a large family (vv 19-22). Jeroboam, on the other hand, is struck down by God himself (v 20).

Judah's next king, Asa, is regarded very highly by the writer of Kings, who remarks that he "was wholly true to the Lord all his days" (1 Kgs 15:14). However, the Chronicler found in the Kings account three elements needing explanation: (1) it is noted he had war with Baasha of Israel (1 Kgs 15:16), (2) he made a treaty with Ben-hadad of Damascus (foreign alliances are always considered a violation of faith in God), and (3) in his old age, Asa had sore feet (1 Kgs 15:23). To adjust this material to his understanding of rewards and punishments, the Chronicler characteristically divides Asa's reign into two separate periods.

The first period builds upon the statement of Kings that Asa's heart "was wholly true to Yahweh all his days" (1 Kgs 15:14). The reforming activity mentioned in Kings is expanded and includes the removal of high places in Judah and in portions of the north as well (2 Chr 14:3; 15:8). Other signs of Asa's prosperity are also added. Four times it is stated that the land "had rest" under him (1 Chr 14:1, 6-7; 15:7). Asa's building operations are named (2 Chr 14:6-7), and he is victorious in an otherwise unknown battle against Zerah the Ethiopian, which also serves as the occasion for a prophetic speech by Azariah. This speech is replete with the terminology of retribution:

"Yahweh is with you, while you are with him. If you seek him, he will be found by you, but if you forsake him, he will forsake you. For a long time Israel was without the true God, and without a teaching priest, and without law; but when in their distress they turned to the Lord, the God of Israel, and sought him, he was found by them. In those times there was no peace to him who went out or to him who came in, for great disturbances afflicted all the inhabitants of the lands. They were broken in pieces, nation against nation and city against city, for God troubled them with every sort of distress. But you, take courage! Do not let your hands be weak, for your work shall be rewarded." (2 Chr 15:2-7 RSV)

With such prophetic encouragement, a second round of reforming activities then follows (15:8-18). Idols are removed in both north and south, and mention is made of sojourners from Ephraim, Manasseh, and Simeon who deserted to Asa in Jerusalem when they saw "Yahweh was with him" (15:9). The covenant ceremony climaxing the reforms in Jerusalem includes the provision that "whoever would not seek Yahweh, the God of Israel, should be put to death . . . " (15:13). The Chronicler's own termination of the account continues:

And all Judah rejoiced over the oath; for they had sworn with all their heart, and had sought him with their whole desire, and he was found by them, and Yahweh gave them rest round about. (v 15 RSV)

It is an oddity of the Chronicler's style that, despite other alterations in his account, he regularly retains the expressed evaluation of DH. Verse 17, dependent upon 1 Kings 15:14, states that the high places were *not* taken away out of Israel. While these seeming contradictions may be due to the work of a later editor, they are so common as to suggest that the Chronicler himself has simply not cared to extend his editorial work to that detail.

However, DH included in a matter-of-fact way an account of Asa's undated alliance with Ben-hadad of Syria against Baasha of Israel. Chronicles never allows such a foreign alliance to pass without condemnation, since it represents for him a lack of faith in Yahweh. The Chronicler presents the prophet Hanani to condemn Asa in the thirty-sixth year of his reign. His pronouncement of retribution, predicting continuous wars for Asa as the outcome of this faithlessness, results in a show of Asa's anger both against the prophet and against the people. The description is once again general and rather colorless: "And Asa inflicted cruelties upon some of the people at the same time" (2 Chr 16:10 RSV). The reference to Asa's diseased feet (2 Chr 16:12 = 1 Kgs 15:23) follows, with the notation added that even when his disease was severe, Asa did not seek Yahweh, but sought help from doctors instead.

In summary, three particular aspects of Chronicles' handling of the Asa account are instructive:

1. The Chronicler accepts the basic evaluation of DH as his own, as is almost always the case. The only exceptions are Solomon and Abijah.

2. Chronicles again divides the reign of a given king into two or more periods depending upon the details available from Kings and from an assessment of those details. Thus the doctrine of retribution is applied not only to the reign of a given king as a whole, but to each element within it as well.

3. In cases such as that of Asa, to whom the Chronicler is quite favorably disposed, religious zeal is normally demonstrated very early and for a prolonged period of the king's reign.[1]

Aspects of this doctrine of retribution could be demonstrated from the reign of almost every king of Judah who follows.[2] However, for our purposes it will be sufficient to note several particularly striking examples of the author's style.

Uzziah and Ahaz

Kings had reported briefly that Uzziah—also named Azariah—did what was right, reigned fifty-two years, but died a leper (2 Kgs 14:21-22; 15:1-7). Perhaps in view of his extremely long reign, which would of itself be considered a sign of God's blessing, Chronicles adds examples of his prosperity and notes that his prosperity was the result of his seeking God (see p. 81) in the days of a certain Zechariah, who is surely meant to be understood as a priest. This prosperity includes building operations, victory in warfare, a large army, fame, and strength (2 Chr 26:6-15). To explain Uzziah's leprosy, Chronicles adds in verses 16-20 Uzziah's anger at Azariah and his fellow priests when they warned him not to enter the temple precincts to burn incense. As a result, Uzziah is smitten by God and dies a leper.

A second example involves King Ahaz, the worst of the kings according to DH (2 Kgs 16). Chronicles again adds to the account specific statements and examples of negative retribution:

> God gave him into the hand of the king of Syria, who defeated him and took captive a great number of his people and brought them to Damascus. He was also given into the hand of the king of Israel, who defeated him. . . . For Pekah the son of Remaliah slew a hundred and twenty thousand in Judah in one day, all of them men of valor, because they had forsaken the Lord, the God of their fathers. (2 Chr 28:5-6 RSV)

After Ahaz's appeal to Assyria for help, which the Chronicler again considered evidence of a lack of faith (2 Chr 28:16 = 2 Kgs 16:7a), Chronicles again adds specific examples of attacks upon and defeats of Judah (2 Chr 28:17-18). This explanation is offered of these events: "For the Lord brought Judah low because of Ahaz king of Israel, for he had dealt wantonly in Judah and had been faithless to Yahweh" (v 19 RSV). Ahaz even appealed to the gods of Syria for help, "but they were the ruin of him, and of all Israel" (v 23). The statements of verse 24 are surely meant to be a kind of negative climax to Judah's history. Judah now found itself as evil as its brothers and sisters in the north (who had at least listened to the words of a true prophet of the Lord, vv 8-15):

And Ahaz gathered together the vessels of the house of God and cut in pieces the vessels of the house of God, and he *shut up the doors of the house of the Lord*; and he made himself altars in every corner of Jerusalem. In every city of Judah he made high places to burn incense to other gods, provoking to anger the Lord, the God of his fathers. (2 Chr 28:24-25 RSV, italics added)

Hezekiah

Hezekiah, with Josiah, is among the kings most in favor with DH. He indicates this not only by stating that they "did what was right" (2 Kgs 18:3; 22:2), but also in ascribing to them the removal of the idolatrous high places erected by Solomon, which were the cause of the rending of the northern kingdom from Solomon's son Rehoboam (1 Kgs 11:1-13). The positive significance of Hezekiah for Chronicles is seen first of all in the length of the account of his reign (2 Chr 29-32), but also in the specific kinds of activities engaged in by Hezekiah and the blessings attributed to him.[3] It is he who in the *first* month of the *first* year of his reign (2 Chr 29:3) reopens the doors of the temple closed by the faithless Ahaz. Hezekiah's speech to the Levites at the beginning of his reforming work is again replete with explicit statements of retribution theology:

"Hear me, Levites! Now sanctify yourselves, and sanctify the house of Yahweh, the God of your fathers, and carry out the filth from the holy place. For our fathers *have been unfaithful* and *have done what was evil* in the sight of Yahweh our God; *they have forsaken him*, and have turned away their faces from the habitation of Yahweh, and turned their backs. They also shut the doors of the vestibule and put out the lamps, and have not burned incense or offered burnt offerings in the holy place to the God of Israel. Therefore the *wrath of Yahweh came on Judah and Jerusalem,* and he has made them an object of horror, of astonishment, and of hissing, as you see with your own eyes. For lo, our fathers have fallen by the sword and our sons and our daughters and our wives are in captivity for this." (2 Chr 29:5-9 RSV, italics added)

The remainder of the chapter recounts Hezekiah's restoration of the temple worship, including especially the reordering of the Levites (vv 10-36).

Other specific activities attributed to Hezekiah include an invitation to the separated brethren of the north to join them in keeping the Passover in Jerusalem, an invitation which was accepted, it should be noted, by many northerners (2 Chr 30:18-25). It was probably this participation of the north which occasioned the Chronicler's statement concluding the festivities:

So there was great joy in Jerusalem, for *since the time of Solomon the son of David king of Israel* there had been nothing like this in Jerusalem. (v 26 RSV, italics added)

After the account of additional reforms in both north and south (2 Chr 31:1) and in the temple (vv 2-19), Chronicles concludes the reforming activity of Hezekiah with the words:

Thus Hezekiah did throughout all Judah; and he did what was good and right and faithful before the Lord his God. And every work that he undertook in the service of the house of God and in accordance with the law and the commandments, seeking his God, he did with all his heart, and prospered. (vv 20-21 RSV)

A similar statement of retributive blessing stands at the end of Chronicles' account of Hezekiah's engagement with Sennacherib of Assyria. An introductory phrase, "after these things and these acts of faithfulness . . . ," places this encounter within the context of Hezekiah's faithfulness (2 Chr 32:1a), and here too Hezekiah's words to his troops are reminiscent of those of a prophet:

> "Be strong and of good courage. Do not be afraid or dismayed before the king of Assyria and all the horde that is with him; for there is one greater with us than with him. With him is an arm of flesh; but with us is Yahweh our God, to help us and to fight our battles." (vv 7-8 RSV)

The writer's praise of Hezekiah reaches its climax after the victory from that same battle. Characteristic features of blessing abound:

> So the Lord saved Hezekiah and the inhabitants of Jerusalem from the hand of Sennacherib king of Assyria and from the hand of all his enemies; and he *gave them rest* on every side. And many *brought gifts* to Yahweh to Jerusalem and *precious things* to Hezekiah king of Judah, so that he *was exalted in the sight of all nations* from that time onward. (2 Chr 32:22-23 RSV, italics added)

Unfortunately, Kings had also reported the sickness of Hezekiah (2 Kgs 20:1). His breach of faith in the matter of the Babylonian envoys is admitted by Chronicles, but covered over with the prosaic and nonspecific vocabulary regularly found in such instances (cf. 2 Kgs 12:7-8, 12):

> But Hezekiah did not make return according to the benefit done to him, for his heart was proud. Therefore

wrath came upon him and Judah and Jerusalem. But Hezekiah *humbled himself* for the pride of his heart, both he and the inhabitants of Jerusalem, so that *the wrath of Yahweh* did not come upon them in the days of Hezekiah. (2 Chr 32:25-26 RSV, italics added)

It is surely a sign of the writer's boundless praise for Hezekiah that, despite such a negative note at the end of his reign, there nevertheless follows an addition from the Chronicler's hand pointing to his riches, honor, building operations, and general prosperity (vv 27-30). To my knowledge, such a situation does not occur elsewhere in the book.

Manasseh and Josiah

The reign of Manasseh is similarly divided into two periods. The material provided Chronicles by DH in the case of Manasseh presented a difficult problem. Manasseh is judged as completely evil, as a result of whose sins Judah would be destroyed without remnant (2 Kgs 21). And yet he had the longest reign of any king of Israel, fifty-five years! Accordingly, Chronicles appends to the Kings account the story of Manasseh's punishment (2 Chr 33:11) and subsequent repentance (vv 12-13, 19; see p. 103). Following that repentance, Manasseh's reign is characterized by the customary blessings: building operations and religious reforms. Noteworthy is the fact that, despite this radical change in the report concerning Manasseh, that of his son Amon which follows nevertheless states that "he did what was evil in the sight of Yahweh, as Manasseh his father had done" (v 22 RSV), although without his father's repentance (v 23).

The account of Josiah also presented our writer with a problem. Josiah's reign, of course, marks the high point of DH's history of Judah. However, 2 Kings 23:29 reports his death in battle at the hands of Necho of Egypt. Chronicles therefore inserts a cause for such a defeat and death: Josiah had disobeyed a command of God given him through the Eqyptian pharaoh (2 Chr 35:21-23). His death, therefore, is in keeping with the general principle of retribution: Blessing follows obedience, and punishment follows disobedience. And the greatest disobedience is failure to hear the voice of Yahweh, even if from the mouth of a foreign ruler.

The last kings of Judah

Judah's end is told in Chronicles in a very sketchy way following the death of Josiah. Jehoiakim, Jehoiachin, and Zedekiah all "did what was evil" in the eyes of Yahweh (2 Chr 36:5, 9, 12), as reported also in Kings. Concerning Zedekiah it is added that "he did not humble himself (i.e., repent) before Jeremiah the prophet, who spoke from the mouth of the Lord" (2 Chr 36:12), and that he violated an oath given to King Nebuchadnezzar "who had made him swear by God" (v 13). Chronicles adds as a final summary of Judah's unfaithfulness:

All the leading priests and the people likewise were exceedingly unfaithful, following all the abominations of the nations; and they polluted the house of Yahweh which he had hallowed in Jerusalem. (v 14 RSV)

Judah's final and ultimate sin, however, which seals her destruction, is that of failure to repent at the preaching of the prophets:

Yahweh, the God of their fathers, sent persistently to them by his messengers, because he had compassion on his people and on his dwelling place; but they kept mocking the messengers of God, despising his words, and scoffing at his prophets, till the wrath of Yahweh

1, 2 CHRONICLES

rose against his people, till there was no remedy. (2 Chr 36:15-16 RSV)

As a result the temple is destroyed, its vessels carried to Babylon, and the land left barren "until the land enjoyed its sabbaths" (2 Chr 36:21), a final punishment which is perhaps at the same time viewed as a purification necessary for God's subsequent redeeming activity.

It thus seems clear that Chronicles has adopted the dogma of retribution, personal and immediate as well as communal and prolonged, as the framework into which the lives of the various kings are fitted, and has regularly added whatever details were necessary to make each individual fit into this scheme. Opinions vary as to whether these additions are based on historical data available to the writer but subsequently lost, or whether, as seems more likely to me, they were logical deductions based on the writer's theology.

Seeking and forsaking God

The two contrasting terms used most frequently throughout Chronicles for presentation of this dogma are those introduced in 1 Chronicles 28:9, "to seek" (dāraš), and "to forsake" ('āzab). It is readily apparent that for Chronicles, which uses the term some forty times, dāraš entails much more than its common translation, "to inquire of." Instead, dāraš is a more general term, including all that might be involved in "keeping the faith" and thus remaining true to Yahweh (cf. 2 Chr 12:14; 14:3; 15:12; 30:19). Similarly, 'āzab and its near synonym, mā'al, "to act unfaithfully," are the most general of terms. The Chronicler's addendum following Saul's death significantly parallels his unfaithfulness and his failure to "seek" Yahweh (1 Chr 10:13-14).

To further define the content of this "seeking" is difficult. That it involved a commitment may be seen from its frequent occurrence in such phrases as "to set (hēkîm) the heart to seek Yahweh," as well as in various covenant contexts where the decision of the people for Yahweh would be of primary importance. That such seeking demanded the avoidance of foreign gods is explicit in such passages as 2 Chronicles 17:3 and 25:15, 20. That it required a positive relationship to the Jerusalem temple might be assumed, and is explicit in at least one case (2 Chr 20:3–4). That this "seeking" involved observable conduct of a certain sort is clear from the account of Asa's covenant, where those who do not seek Yahweh are to be put to death (2 Chr 15:12–13), although in only one instance is this seeking explicitly related to the observance of the Law (2 Chr 17:4).

The emphasis upon faith and commitment is strongly accented. Two aspects of the Chronicler's presentation stand in bold relief: (1) In numerous cases the need for complete reliance on Yahweh is given extended treatment, both in various prophetic speeches as well as in the editorial framework of the book. The key word often found in such a context is šā'an, "to rely upon" (cf. 2 Chronicles 13:18; 14:10; 16:7–8).

A similar point is made in Jehoshaphat's address to his troops prior to their engagement with the Moabites. There, Jehoshaphat's words "Believe (Heb. 'mn, hiphil) in Yahweh your God, and you will be established; believe his prophets, and you will succeed" (2 Chr 20:20) recall Isaiah's demand for faith in the face of the Syro-Ephraimitic encounter (Isa 7:9). In this victory, as in numerous others, Israel's victory is assured when she has shown the necessary faith; the narration of the battle is couched in terms often reminiscent of the holy war, again recalling Isaiah. In further agreement with Isaiah, Chronicles regularly looks upon any type of foreign alliance as a sign of apostasy from Yahweh (cf. 2 Chr 16:7; 20:37).

The positive side of the doctrine of retribution is that prosperity results when the proper relationship with God exists. The Chronicler has introduced this important element, too, in David's first speech to Solomon (1 Chr 22:11, 13), which is ultimately dependent upon Joshua 1. The note of prosperity reoccurs in 1 Chronicles 29:23, where it is used to describe Solomon's reign even before it has begun.

The key word of Chronicles in this regard is the causative active (hiphil) of ṣlḥ, "to prosper," which he uses eleven times without precedent in DH. (Ṣlḥ is used in the hiphil only five times in the entire Deuteronomic corpus: Deuteronomy 28:29; Joshua 1:8; Judges 18:5; and 1 Kings 22:12, 15.) But the full significance of the writer's use of this term is apparent only from observing its distribution throughout Chronicles. The Chronicler has reserved the prosperity denoted by this term for precisely that group of kings to whom he is most favorably disposed: Solomon (2 Chr 7:11), Asa (2 Chr 14:6), Jehoshaphat (2 Chr 20:20), Uzziah (2 Chr 26:5), and Hezekiah (2 Chr 31:21). Directly in the case of Uzziah and Hezekiah, and somewhat less directly with Asa, this prosperity is related to the seeking of Yahweh. The reign of Hezekiah, the post-Solomonic king most in favor with Chronicles, is aptly concluded with the words, "Hezekiah *prospered* in all his works" (2 Chr 32:30).

In several cases also the breach of this relationship with God is cited as the actual or potential cause for a lack of prosperity. Abijah's important discourse points out that it is impossible for the north to "succeed" in its war with Judah since God is with Judah and Israel is accordingly fighting against God (2 Chr 13:12). Zechariah's words following Judah's apostasy after the death of the priest Jehoiada also point out the impossibility of Judah's success when she has transgressed Yahweh's commandments and thereby is forsaken (2 Chr 24:20). The statement concluding the first part of Uzziah's reign, "as long as he [Uzziah] *sought* the Lord, God made him *prosper*" (2 Chr 26:5), clearly foreshadows the second part of Uzziah's life when he was unfaithful in entering the temple to burn incense.

Divine Retribution

The marks of prosperity

The many and varied ways in which the Chronicler portrays the prosperous nature of the reigns of God-pleasing kings is one of the most striking characteristics of his account and is highly reminiscent of the recital of covenant blessings and curses found in such passages as Deuteronomy 27 and 28.

First it is, for example, frequently stated of the godly king that Yahweh was "with him" (Solomon, 2 Chr 1:1; Judah at the time of Abijah, 2 Chr 13:12; Jehoshaphat, 2 Chr 17:3; Asa, 2 Chr 15:9). Echoes of this ancient formulation also occur, although modified by their inclusion in larger literary forms or under the influence of the Chronicler's theology. Hence, variations of the statement are applied to Jehoshaphat (2 Chr 20:17), Hezekiah (2 Chr 32:8), and perhaps Pharaoh Neco (2 Chr 35:21) in the context of "holy war." Its use by David in 1 Chronicles 22:11 in an imperfect (jussive) form, "may Yahweh be with you," as well as by Jehoshaphat in 2 Chronicles 19:6, is probably influenced by connections with the form used for induction of an official to an office.[4] The conditional formulation in 2 Chronicles 15:2, "Yahweh is with you, while you are with him," is an obvious alteration of the standard phrase under the influence of the Chronicler's doctrine of retribution.

Secondly, the concept of "rest" ($m^e n\hat{u}h\bar{a}h$), introduced by the Chronicler in 1 Chronicles 22:9, is afterward applied to various other periods in Judah's history to point to the peace or rest attending a God-pleasing reign. (For other aspects of the "rest" theme, see chapter 8.) This is most apparent in the description of the first part of Asa's reign, where three occurrences of the Hebrew "to rest" ($n\hat{u}ah$), are joined with one of "quietness" ($\check{s}\bar{a}qat$):

> . . . Asa his son reigned in his stead. In his days the
> land *had rest* for ten years. And Asa did what was good

and right in the eyes of Yahweh his God. . . . And
the kingdom *had rest* under him. He built fortified
cities in Judah, for the land *had rest.* He had *no war* in
those years, for Yahweh gave him *peace.* And he said to
Judah, "Let us build these cities, and surround them
with walls and towers, gates and bars; the land is still
ours, because we have sought Yahweh our God; we
have sought him, and he has *given us peace* on every
side." So they built and prospered. (2 Chr 14:1–2, 5b–7
RSV; Heb. 13:23, 14:4b–6, italics added)

Both *hēnîaḥ* and *šāqaṭ* are used to describe a portion of
Jehoshaphat's reign (2 Chr 20:30). Concerning Hezekiah,
Chronicles concludes by adding to a narrative generally
taken from Kings the phrase, "Yahweh . . . *gave them rest*
on every side" (2 Chr 32:22).

Chronicles has also pointed out the prosperity which belonged to the reigns of God-pleasing kings in numerous
other specific ways. In most of these, it appears that the
description of the unprecedented prosperity of Solomon's
reign as presented in Kings and repeated by Chronicles has
been used as a basis. Thus Chronicles repeats the tradition
of Solomon's riches (1 Kgs 3:12–13; 10:22 = 2 Chr 1:12–13;
10:22) and applies it also to Jehoshaphat (2 Chr 17:5) and
Hezekiah (2 Chr 32:27). The closely related honor and fame
are likewise marks of Solomon in both 1 Kings 3:12–13 and
2 Chronicles 1:12, but the Chronicler inserts a similar notice into his account of David (1 Chr 17:17), Jehoshaphat
(2 Chr 17:5), Uzziah (2 Chr 26:8, 15), and Hezekiah (2 Chr
32:27). Statements that a king became great or strong are
common, beginning again with Solomon (2 Chr 1:1) and
continuing with Rehoboam (2 Chr 11:17), Abijah (2 Chr
13:21), Jehoshaphat (2 Chr 17:1, 5, 11), Uzziah (2 Chr 26:8,
15), and Jotham (2 Chr 27:6).

The large armies of various kings are referred to as evident

Divine Retribution   85 testimony of their prosperity and strength (2 Chr 13:3; 14:8; 17:3-19; 26:11-15), as are the victories they achieve in battle (Abijah—2 Chr 13:13-20; Asa—2 Chr 14:12-15; Jehoshaphat—2 Chr 20:1-30; Amaziah—2 Chr 25:11-13; Jotham—2 Chr 26:7; Hezekiah—2 Chr 32:22).

For David, see 1 Chronicles 18:1-20:8. Particular notice should be taken that in this almost complete list of Chronicles' favorite kings, Solomon, the "man of peace," is noticeably absent. Terminology of the holy war is again present in relating that the "fear of Yahweh" fell upon the surrounding nations during the reigns of Asa, Jehoshaphat, and David (2 Chr 14:14; 17:10; 20:29; 1 Chr 14:17).

Another method used to demonstrate the prosperity of God-pleasing kings is in reporting the building activities undertaken during the God-pleasing portions of their reigns. While many of these are related to the temple and its environs (2 Chr 15:8; 24:4; 27:3; 29:3; 33:17 [of Manasseh!]; 34:8-15 = 2 Kgs 22:3-6), an equal number are concerned with all kinds of secular building operations, including fortifications. Note again the comprehensive nature of the list: Solomon (2 Chr 8:2-6); Rehoboam (2 Chr 11:5-12); Asa (2 Chr 14:5); Uzziah (2 Chr 26:6-8); Jehoshaphat (2 Chr 17:12); Jotham (2 Chr 27:3); and Hezekiah (2 Chr 32:8, 28-30)!

It is also stated by Chronicles that the kings of the world brought gifts, not only to Solomon (2 Chr 9:23 = 1 Kgs 10:23), but also to Jehoshaphat (2 Chr 17:11), Uzziah (2 Chr 26:8), and Hezekiah (2 Chr 32:23) as well. In the last case, the gifts brought to Hezekiah are paralleled with those brought to Yahweh.

It is accordingly clear that the writer of Chronicles has gone to great lengths to describe the prosperity enjoyed by God-pleasing kings in accordance with his understanding of divine retribution. In a few cases these elements are already present in the Chronicler's presentation of David, but in most the prosperity attending Solomon's reign as presented in Kings has been adopted by Chronicles and used as a model to describe the reigns of post-Solomonic kings.

Forsaking Yahweh

The negative counterpart of "seeking" Yahweh is represented generally by the verb "to forsake" (*'āzab*), and the root *m'l*, "to act unfaithfully." This apostasy is often very general in nature, as indicated in instances where Chronicles, after recounting a section from Kings which details a king's wicked practices, concludes with a generalizing phrase such as "because they had forsaken the Lord" (2 Chr 21:10; 28:6). But at other times this "forsaking" is more closely defined by the context as referring to such transgressions as failure to observe the law (2 Chr 12:1, 5) or idol worship (2 Chr 24:18; 7:22 = 1 Kgs 9:9).

Forsaking Yahweh most commonly involves the relationship of the individual to the Jerusalem temple. This is assured by the account surrounding Jehoiada's death, when Judah "*forsook* the house of Yahweh . . . and served the Asherim and the idols" (2 Chr 24:18), as well as by the summary of the apostasy preceding Hezekiah's reform:

> For our fathers *have been unfaithful* and have done what was evil in the sight of Yahweh our God; they have *forsaken* him, and have turned away their faces from the habitation of Yahweh, and turned their backs. They also shut the doors of the vestibule and put out the lamps, and have not burned incense or offered burnt offerings in the holy place to the God of Israel. (2 Chr 29:6-7 RSV, italics added)

The relationship between this unfaithfulness to and forsaking of Yahweh and the cult is also seen in the programmatic speech of Abijah in 2 Chronicles 13, which expresses the Chronicler's judgment upon the northern tribes. The statement that the north has forsaken Yahweh (2 Chr 13:11) is preceded by an account which specifically mentions the expulsion of the Aaronites and Levites from their offices by Jeroboam (v 9). On the other hand, the south can affirm that it has *not* forsaken Yahweh, since the legitimate priesthood still serves there, together with the prescribed temple services which include such minutiae as the daily offering of the shewbread and the lighting of the golden lampstands (2 Chr 13:9-12).

Forms of the verb "to act unfaithfully" (the root m'l), are familiar from the priestly vocabulary of the Pentateuch and such works as Ezekiel. They occur some sixteen times in 2 Chronicles and appear even more general in the viewpoint expressed than does 'āzab. This can be seen from the summary manner in which the root is used to describe the reigns of Ahaz (2 Chr 28:19, compare 29:6) and Manasseh (2 Chr 33:19), as well as Judah's condition which ultimately led to the Exile (2 Chr 36:14, compare 1 Chr 5:25; 9:1). At times, however, this "unfaithfulness" has direct reference to one's relationship to the temple (2 Chr 26:16, 18; 36:14). In sharp contrast, all five occurrences of the root m'l in Ezra and Nehemiah deal with the problem of foreign marriages, providing additional evidence that those books do not stem from the same author(s) as Chronicles.[5]

As might be expected in view of the details with which Chronicles has described the prosperity resulting from "seeking" Yahweh, the results of unfaithfulness to God are also presented in considerable variety and detail. Forsaking Yahweh results in war (2 Chr 16:9; 21:6), defeat (2 Chr 24:23-24; 25:17-24; 28:6, 19; 30:7), disease (2 Chr 16:12; 21:14, 18; 26:19), and conspiracy (2 Chr 24:25; 25:27). That the details themselves are rather insignificant for the Chronicler can be seen from the fact that he is quite commonly content to describe the results with the equally general phrase that "wrath" came, or did not come, upon the offending party (2 Chr 12:7, 12; 19:2; 32:26). To forsake Yahweh means simply to be cast off or forsaken by him, with all his blessings (1 Chr 28:9). While Yahweh is *with* those who seek him, he is *not with* those who are unfaithful to him (2 Chr 13:12).

In only one case does it appear that Chronicles has failed to carry the dogma of retribution through to its complete and logical conclusion without mention of repentance (see pp. 100–04). King Jehoshaphat, for whom the Chronicler shows great sympathy, is rebuked by the seer Hanani for his alliance with Ahab of Israel. And it is reported that "wrath has gone out against you from Yahweh" as a result (2 Chr 19:2). However, this rebuke is immediately tempered with the note that "some good" was found in him, since he had destroyed the Asherahs from the land (v 3).

In summary, then, we may conclude that the doctrine of retribution is by all accounts *the* principle governing the Chronicler's presentation of the post-Solomonic kings. The great majority of the alterations, additions, and deletions to the text of Kings made by Chronicles are easily explicable on the basis of this single teaching. In that light, it is surprising that for Chronicles retribution is not the final word.

*　　*　　*

Retribution in the New Testament is both affirmed and denied. On the one hand the chief teaching of the Christian faith is that people are unable to merit God's approval by their good deeds, and hence are justified only by God's grace through faith in Christ Jesus. Even faith, the apostle Paul affirms, is not to be considered a meritorious work, but is itself a gift of God (Eph 2:8). On the other hand, the value and necessity of good works is repeatedly affirmed. God's people are created for good works (Eph 2:10), and faith always produces good works. In fact, "faith" which does not produce good works is really no faith at all (James 2:17). In that light, final judgment can be affirmed to be based upon works. Those who will inherit the kingdom are those who have fed the hungry, given drink to the thirsty, welcomed the stranger, clothed the naked, and visited the sick and imprisoned (Matt 25:34–36). Their faith has borne fruit, resulting in that loving obedience which is the mark of God's people.

7

THE PERFECT HEART

---

*And the people rejoiced over their generous contributions,
for it was with a perfect heart that they had made these
generous contributions to Yahweh; David the king also
rejoiced with great joy.* (1 Chr 29:9)

Studies of Chronicles are frequently less than sympathetic, and are apt to point to the concern for temple and
priesthood, and the emphasis upon required participation
in temple worship in a quite rigid and colorless way. To do
so, however, is to miss a vital part of the Chronicler's emphasis: The people of God participate in these and other
God-pleasing activities with wholehearted dedication, generosity, and joy, because their participation flows from
hearts that are pure and undivided in loyalty to Yahweh.
The result for Chronicles is a book permeated by unity,
gratitude, enthusiasm, and exultation.

This oneness of mind and intent is seen already in the
concept of "all Israel." It is important for the author that
the people of God are *one people*, unified not only in their

The Perfect Heart 91

loyalty to Yahweh but in their activities undertaken in his name.

But this unity of heart and mind is also an internal thing. Individual Israelites also are to be marked by attitudes and actions that flow from single, perfect, undivided hearts.

This is first seen in the words with which the Chronicler has concluded his account of the troops who came to Hebron to make David king. They came to Hebron with a "perfect heart" (Heb. *lēbāb šālēm*) to make David king (1 Chr 12:39). All the rest of Israel, too, is of *a single heart* (Heb. *lēb 'eḥad*) to make David king. David exhorts Solomon to serve Yahweh with "a perfect heart and a willing spirit" (1 Chr 28:9) and includes a prayer that Solomon may keep God's commandments with a whole heart (29:19), for Yahweh is the one who searches every heart and understands every thought (28:9).

This linkage of heart and mind is also found in 2 Chronicles 6:38, 15:12, and 34:31, where the contexts are appropriately repentance, seeking the Lord, and obeying his law. The perfect heart is in 2 Chronicles 19:9 identified with faithfulness, and that of course is the disposition which the Chronicler is seeking to express.

Other expressions are also frequent. Israelites are to give generously from an upright and perfect heart (2 Chr 29:17). They are to return to Yahweh with all the heart (2 Chr 16:38), seek Yahweh with all the heart (22:9), and act with all the heart that they might prosper (31:21).

It is striking that Chronicles does not state in so many words that either David or Solomon served God perfectly. This is, however, affirmed of the remainder of the kings with whom the Chronicler was particularly pleased—Asa (2 Chr 15:17 = 1 Kgs 15:14), Jehoshaphat (2 Chr 22:9), Hezekiah (2 Chr 31:21), and Josiah (2 Chr 34:31 = 2 Kgs 23:3).

In the frequency of his usage of the phrase "with *all* the heart" the writer is probably once again dependent upon the format provided him by DH; however, with characteristic style he has expanded and deepened that emphasis.

Joy as an expression of a perfect heart

The same is true concerning expressions of joy in Chronicles. In 2 Kings 8:66 Solomon dedicates the temple with great joy and gladness of heart. Chronicles captures this attitude and repeats it on numerous appropriate occasions. For example, the feast following David's acceptance as king in Hebron by all Israel is marked with such elaborate joy and feasting that some have seen in it a messianic, or even eschatological, element:

> All these, men of war, arrayed in battle order, came to Hebron with full intent to make David king over all Israel; likewise all the rest of Israel were of a single mind to make David king. And they were there with David for three days, eating and drinking, for their brethren had made preparation for them. And also their neighbors, from as far as Issachar and Zebulun and Naphtali, came bringing food on asses and on camels and on mules and on oxen, abundant provisions of meal, cakes of figs, clusters of raisins, and wine and oil, oxen and sheep, for there was joy in Israel. (1 Chr 12:38-40, Heb. vv 39-41)

This note of joy returns at appropriate points throughout the books. The transfer of the ark of the covenant to Jerusalem is attended by great joy in Chronicles (1 Chr 15:25-28) as in DH (2 Sam 6:12-15), although the sacral nature of the festivity is more pronounced in Chronicles. The presence of the Levites with their musical instruments must have added substantially to the festivities in the writer's mind. The association of the Levites and singers with such joy will be marked again: 1 Chr 15:16, 2 Chr 23:18, and 29:30.

This note of joyous eating and drinking is also found in David's gathering of the assembly in 1 Chronicles 29:22, when the assembly "ate and drank before the Lord . . . with great gladness," and at the dedication of the temple in 2 Chronicles 7:10. In this last case the reference is taken from 1 Kings 8:66, although, as is often the case, Chronicles has added additional emphasis to his source by lengthening the duration of the feast:

> At that time Solomon kept the feast seven days, and all Israel with him, a very great congregation, from the entrance of Hamath to the Brook of Egypt. And on the eighth day they held a solemn assembly; for they had kept the dedication of the altar seven days and the feast seven days. On the twenty-third day of the seventh month he sent the people away to their homes, joyful and glad of heart for the goodness that Yahweh had shown to David and to Solomon and to Israel his people. (2 Chr 7:8–10)

In the remainder of Chronicles, the covenant of Asa (2 Chr 15:15) and Joash's reform (2 Chr 24:10) occasion this kind of joy. Above all, however, it is repeatedly mentioned in conjunction with Hezekiah's Passover, when the celebration is again lengthened to fourteen days and we are reminded, "there was great joy in Jerusalem, for since the time of Solomon the son of David king of Israel there had been nothing like this in Jerusalem" (2 Chr 30:26; cf. vv 21, 23). One of the stronger arguments for the unity of Chronicles and Ezra is surely the similarity in tone (and vocabulary) of this account with the story of the laying of the foundation of the temple (Ezra 3:13) and its dedication (Ezra 6:22), where the note of joy is prominent.

A similar attitude expressed repeatedly in Chronicles is that of generosity. This attitude reaches its peak in 1 Chronicles 29, which describes the contributions made by David and Israel's leaders for the construction of the temple. Here alone the verb "to offer freely" occurs no less than six times (vv 5, 6, 9, 14, 17 [twice]):

> I know, my God, that you test the heart, and have pleasure in uprightness. In the uprightness of my heart I have *freely offered* these things, and now I have seen your people, who are present here, *offering freely* and joyously to you. (1 Chr 29:17)

In this single passage, it might be noted, are combined the concepts of uprightness of heart, joy, and generosity. The note of generosity is found again characteristically in 2 Chronicles 31:5, associated with Hezekiah's Passover, and in 35:8, with the Passover of Josiah.

In these cases it is again apparent that Chronicles has been influenced by DH, from whom these themes and attitudes have been "borrowed." In the case of generous offerings, the Chronicler is also dependent upon the tabernacle pericopes of Exodus 25–30 and 35–40. However, he has characteristically magnified both the number of occasions in which he has introduced the theme and the degree of the joy and generosity. The result is a narrative in which the rather routine and prosaic is given warmth and color by people and events which reflect the writer's perception of what life in God's kingdom is to be like. Faithful to him with a perfect heart, their lives are marked by generosity and joy.

The perfect heart in the New Testament

Readers of the New Testament will feel a particularly close and common bond with such passages speaking of uprightness of heart, joy, and generosity. Jesus warns his followers that something more is required than the righteousness of the scribes and Pharisees, which is often portrayed as a righteousness in conformity with external requirements (Matt 5:20). Thus the commandment "you shall not kill" is violated not only by those who murder, but by those who are angry and hate (Matt 5:21-22), and the person who looks upon a woman lustfully commits adultery (Matt 5:27-28). Works of piety are not performed to be seen by people, but are matters between God and his people (Matt 6:1-8). It is the pure in heart who will see God (Matt 5:8). Examples could be multiplied.

The New Testament is also a book of generosity and compassion. God, Paul affirms simply and directly, loves a cheerful giver (2 Cor 9:7). It is the merciful who will receive mercy (Matt 5:7); he who sows bountifully will reap bountifully (2 Cor 9:6). God's people will be enriched for great generosity (2 Cor 9:11), and are given the promise that they will always have enough of everything for their own needs and for every good work as well (2 Cor 9:8).

The message of joy in the Lord is still another theme which the New Testament carries forward. A few examples will suffice to point the interested reader in the proper direction. The angel of the Lord who appears to the shepherds to announce the birth of Jesus says:

"Be not afraid; for behold, I bring you good news of a *great joy* which will come to all the people; for to you is born this day in the city of David a Savior, who is Christ the Lord." (Luke 2:10-11 RSV, emphasis added)

Jesus' parables of the Lost Sheep and the Lost Coin speak of the joy among the angels of heaven over a single sinner who repents (Luke 15:1-10). And the parable of the Prodigal Son, which might better be named the parable of the

Two Lost Sons, is surely meant to condemn those who find no joy in the repentance of a lost brother (Luke 15:11-32). Joy is listed second, preceded only by love, in Paul's listing of those fruits of the Spirit which are to be reflected in the Christian's life (Gal 5:22-23). One New Testament letter, Philippians, is commonly called "the epistle of joy" because of that note which occurs so frequently there (cf. 1:4, 18-19; 2:2, 17-18, 29; 3:1; 4:1, 10, and especially 4:4-7, in which joy is the dominant Christian virtue stemming from God's nearness):

> Rejoice in the Lord always; again I will say, Rejoice. Let all men know your forbearance. The Lord is at hand. Have no anxiety about anything, but in everything by prayer and supplication with thanksgiving let your requests be made known to God. And the peace of God, which passes all understanding, will keep your hearts and your minds in Christ Jesus. (Phil 4:4-7)

8

THE MERCY OF GOD

Many of the people, many of them from Ephraim, Man-
asseh, Issachar, and Zebulun, had not purified them-
selves, but ate the passover in violation of what was
written. But Hezekiah prayed for them, saying: "May
the Good Lord pardon every one who sets his heart to
seek God, Yahweh, God of his fathers, even though not
according to the sanctuary's rules of purity." And Yah-
weh heard Hezekiah, and forgave the people. (2 Chr
30:18-20)

The study of divine retribution points to a detailed correspondence between obedience and prosperity and between
disobedience and punishment, a correspondence which outlines the justice of God in bold terms. It underscores in bold
lines the preachment of the Law: "'You shall be holy; for I,
Yahweh your God am holy'" (Lev 19:2) and, "'You shall have
no other gods before me'" (Exod 20:3). And, such a study
points to the God who will "by no means clear the guilty,
visiting the iniquity of the fathers upon the children and the

children's children, to the third and the fourth generation" (Exod 34:7).

But the Chronicler also knows of another side of God's nature, prominent in what has almost become a creedal statement in the Old Testament:

"Yahweh, Yahweh, a God merciful and gracious, slow to anger, and abounding in steadfast love and faithfulness, keeping steadfast love for thousands, forgiving iniquity and transgression and sin. . . ." (Exod 34:6-7)

It is this mercy and grace which is celebrated in the response borrowed from the Psalms and incorporated in the text to be sung by the Levites: "O give thanks to Yahweh, for he is good; because his steadfast love (Heb. ḥesed) lasts for ever" (1 Chr 16:34). This same response is repeated by all Israel at the dedication of the temple in words found only in Chronicles (2 Chr 7:3).

One finds God's grace—pure, unmerited love of God—in places we seldom notice. Because of his love God chose Abraham to receive his promise (Gen 12:1-3). That same love led him to keep his promise to Abraham and to choose Israel as his people (Deut 7:7-8), to bring them into the promised land, and to make his promise of an everlasting kingship to David (1 Chr 17).

The Chronicler also knows of a grace of God in the affairs of daily life which surpasses strict retribution and justice and is available through prayer and repentance. While the Chronicler's language is frequently general and even vague here, instances such as that in 2 Chronicles 12:6-12 are clear in their intent. Israel has forsaken God, and has in turn been forsaken by him and given into the hand of Shishak of Egypt. But Chronicles adds:

Then the princes of Israel and the king *humbled them-selves* and said, "The Lord is righteous." When Yahweh saw that they humbled themselves, the word of Yahweh came to Shemaiah: "They have humbled themsleves; I will not destroy them, but I will grant them some deliverance, and my wrath shall not be poured out upon Jerusalem by the hand of Shishak. Nevertheless they shall be servants to him, that they may know my service and the service of the kingdoms of the countries." (2 Chr 12:6-8)

After repeating a segment of Kings recounting Shishak's pillaging of the temple (2 Chr 12:9-11 = 1 Kgs 14:76-28), Chronicles again adds: "When he [Rehoboam] humbled himself the wrath of Yahweh turned from him, so as not to make a complete destruction . . ." (2 Chr 12:12).

The Chronicler cites examples of past repentance for the people's guidance (2 Chr 15:4). Hezekiah's letter assures even the rebellious north that the grace and mercy of God will not permit him to ignore those who turn to him:

"O people of Israel, return to Yahweh, the God of Abraham, Isaac, and Israel, that he may turn again to the remnant of you who have escaped from the hand of the kings of Assyria . . . Do not now be stiff-necked as your fathers were, but yield yourselves to Yahweh, and come to his sanctuary, which he has sanctified for ever, and serve Yahweh your God. . . . For if you return to Yahweh, your brethren and your children will find compassion with their captors, and return to this land. For Yahweh your God is gracious and merciful, and will not turn away his face from you, if you return to him." (2 Chr 30:6, 8-9 RSV)

The Mercy of God

Hezekiah also prays for the pardon of those who ate of his Passover without being able to observe the strict rules of cleanliness: "'The good LORD pardon every one who sets his heart to seek God, Yahweh, the God of his fathers, even though not according to the sanctuary's rules of cleanness'" (2 Chr 30:18-19 RSV). And we are told, "Yahweh heard Hezekiah, and healed the people" (v 20).

Another verse from the account of Hezekiah exemplifies how significant the Chronicler's perception of repentance and grace is for his understanding of Yahweh's dealings with his people:

> In those days Hezekiah became sick and was at the point of death, and he prayed to Yahweh; and he answered him and gave him a sign. But Hezekiah did not make return according to the benefit done to him, for his heart was proud. Therefore wrath came upon him and Judah and Jerusalem. But Hezekiah *humbled himself* for the pride of his heart, both he and the inhabitants of Jerusalem, so that the wrath of Yahweh did not come upon them in the days of Hezekiah." (2 Chr 32:24-26 RSV, italics added)

Josiah's exemption from the punishment coming upon Judah is based upon a similar statement, in this case borrowed from Kings (2 Chr 34:26-28 = 2 Kgs 22:18-22).

Chronicles alone reports that the wicked King Manasseh was deported to Babylon (2 Chr 33:11). But the account continues:

> When he was in distress he entreated the favor of Yahweh his God and *humbled himself* greatly before the God of his fathers. He prayed to him, and God received his entreaty and heard his supplication and brought him

again to Jerusalem into his kingdom. Then Manasseh knew that Yahweh was God. (2 Chr 33:12–13 RSV)

It is probable, as mentioned earlier (p. 79), that the Chronicler was struck by the utter inconsistency of Manasseh's great wickedness and his unparalleled reign of fifty-five years. He concluded, on the basis of his understanding of God's ways, that Manasseh *must* have repented to enjoy such a long reign.

Finally, however, it was Israel's refusal to repent that led to the Exile. Zedekiah would not humble himself before the prophet Jeremiah (2 Chr 36:12), and the priests mocked and scoffed at the prophets until there was no "healing" or forgiveness (vv 15–16). It would require another pure and unmerited act of God's love to stir up Cyrus to proclaim release to his people so that they might return and build him a house in Jerusalem (2 Chr 36:22–23).

* * *

Without minimizing the element of God's justice, the New Testament is above all and from first to last a hymn of praise to the mercy of God and an exhortation to those who would follow him to exhibit that same kind of mercy. The vocabulary here is rich and varied: mercy, grace, love, kindness, compassion, etc. But all point to a God who so loved the world as to give his Son for its salvation (John 3:16).

The Song of Zechariah correctly summarizes the Old Testament promise as "the *mercy* promised to our fathers" (Luke 1:72 RSV, emphasis added), and the words from Isaiah chosen by Jesus for reading in the synagogue in Nazareth as he began his ministry are words which essentially outline a ministry of mercy (Luke 4:18–19).

Jesus is the one who has come to call, not the righteous, but sinners to repentance (Luke 5:32). The self-righteous, who think they are well and need no physician and despise others, reject the ministry of the one who receives sinners and even eats with them. The parable of the Good Samaritan is a parable about mercy. The Good Samaritan showed mercy, and Jesus' hearers are commanded to go and do likewise (Luke 10:29–37). Those who place themselves under God's mercy are those for whom the Messiah came—like the tax collector of another parable (Luke 18:9–14), the ten lepers (Luke 7:11–19), or the blind Bartimaeus, the recovery of whose sight serves as a symbolic opening to the Passion narrative (Mark 10:46–52).

9

THE PROMISED REST

Then [David] called for Solomon his son, and charged
him to build a house for Yahweh, the God of Israel.
David said to Solomon, "My son, I had it in my heart to
build a house for the name of Yahweh my God. But the
word of Yahweh came to me, saying, 'You have shed
much blood and have waged great wars; you shall not
build a house for my name, because you have shed so
much blood before me upon the earth. Behold, a son will
be born to you; he will be a man of rest [Heb. mᵉnûḥâ]. I
will give him rest [Heb. nûḥ hiphil] from all his enemies
round about; for his name shall be Solomon [Heb.
šᵉlōmō], and I will give Israel peace [Heb. šālôm] and
quietness [Heb. šeqet] in his days. He will build a house
for my name, and he will be my son, and I will be his
father, and I will establish the throne of his kingdom
over Israel for ever.'" (1 Chr 22:6–11)

The theme of a divinely provided rest extends from the
earliest to the latest writers of Holy Scripture. Not counting

the Sabbath rest of Genesis 2:1-3, which is of a different sort and belongs to the latest tradition of the Pentateuch—a tradition probably akin in both content and date to that of 2 Chronicles 36:21—the concept of rest is first introduced in association with the ark of the covenant in Numbers 10:33-36. Here we are told that the ark went before the company of Israel a three days' journey to seek out a resting place for Israel. In the apparently ancient poem embedded in verses 35-36 Yahweh's own movements are identified with those of the ark:

> Whenever the ark set out, Moses said, "Arise, O Yahweh, and let thy enemies be scattered; and let them that hate thee flee before thee." And when it rested, he said, "Return, O Yahweh, to the ten thousand thousands of Israel." (Num 10:35-36 RSV)

Of all of the theological motifs developed by the Chronicler, perhaps none is pursued in so striking a manner as that of the concept of rest (verb *nûaḥ*, noun *m'nûḥâ*). This concept is of vital importance for understanding the relationship of David and Solomon, and the relationship of them and the Davidic dynasty to the temple. It becomes at the same time a significant element within his theology of retribution and, finally, is suggestive for the development of a later tradition developed by the New Testament writer of Hebrews.

"Rest" in the Deuteronomistic History

To appreciate the Chronicler's use of the concept of rest it is necessary to review the same concept as it occurs in Deuteronomy and the DH. In Deuteronomy 12, the unification of Israel's worship at a single site was integrally bound up with the nation's *rest* in the promised land:

You shall not do according to all that we are doing here this day, every man doing whatever is right in his own eyes; for you have not as yet come to the rest [m⁺nûḥâ] and to the inheritance which Yahweh your God gives you. But when you go over the Jordan, and live in the land which Yahweh your God gives you to inherit, and when he *gives you rest* from all your enemies round about, so that you live in safety, then to the place where Yahweh your God will choose, to make his name dwell there, thither you shall bring all that I command you: your burnt offerings and your sacrifices, your tithes and the offering that you present, and all your votive offerings which you vow to the Lord. (Deut 12:8–11 RSV)

The Priestly writer (P), too, senses a connection between God-given rest in the promised land and the erection of a single place of worship. After the story of Joshua's conquest of the land is finished in Joshua 11:23 with the statement that "the land had rest from war," the first event recorded by P after the apportioning of the land is the erection of the tent of meeting at Shiloh (Josh 18:1).

The Deuteronomic writers, however, do not apply this principle consistently. Joshua 21:43–45 includes the rest following the conquest of Palestine as indicative of the fulfillment of all God's promises to his people (cf. also Joshua 23:1). However, a similar idea occurs frequently describing the periodic and temporary periods of peace enjoyed by various of Israel's judges (cf. Judg 3:30 and 5:31).

Both the connection between "rest" and temple building and the inconsistency in the use of the motif are seen in DH's account of the dynastic oracle to David in 2 Samuel 7. The oracle begins with the words, "Now when the king dwelt in his house, and Yahweh *had given him rest* from all his enemies round about . . ." (2 Sam 7:1–2). In the oracle which follows, however, it is not David but one of his off-spring who will build the temple (2 Sam 7:12–13).[1] In a later passage (which Chronicles omits in his telling of the story of the temple dedication), DH has Solomon write to King Huram of Tyre:

"You know David my father, that he was not able to build a house for the name of Yahweh his God because of the warfare which surrounded him, until Yahweh subdued them beneath the soles of his feet. But now Yahweh my God has *given me rest* round about. There is no adversary nor evil occurrence. So behold I am planning to build a house for the name of Yahweh my God, as Yahweh spoke to David my father, saying, 'Your son, whom I will put in your place, upon your throne, will build the house for my name.'" (1 Kgs 5:3–5, Heb. 5:17–19)

Here David's failure to build the temple is seen as the natural result of the fact that he was regularly involved in wars, which prevented him from doing so. Thus it has fallen to Solomon to erect the temple. And his blessing pronounced following the dedication of the temple makes clear once again the relationship between God's promises, the conquest of the land, the erection of the temple, and rest:

"Blessed be Yahweh who has *given rest* to his people Israel, according to all that he promised; not one word has failed of all his good promise, which he uttered by Moses his servant. Yahweh our God be with us, as he was with our fathers; may he not leave us or forsake us; that he may incline our hearts to him, to walk in all his ways, and to keep his commandments, his statutes, and his ordinances, which he commanded our fathers." (1 Kgs 8:56–58 RSV)

1, 2 CHRONICLES

"Rest" in Chronicles

The Chronicler, it should be admitted, has omitted *both* of these last two passages from his narrative. He has apparently done this, however, not because he considered them unimportant, but for exactly the opposite reason! He has decided to use them as the theme for his entire account, and has thus chosen to omit them from the narrative by his account.

In the case of David's wars, mentioned by Kings as preventing David from building the temple, Chronicles has heightened David's involvement and made Yahweh's rejection of him as temple builder explicit. David is a "warrior" (1 Chr 28:3), who has "shed much blood and . . . waged great wars" (1 Chr 22:8). Therefore Yahweh himself has explicitly forbidden him to build his temple, and given that task to his son Solomon the "man of peace":

> The word of the Lord came to me [David] saying, "You have shed much blood and have waged great wars; you shall not build a house to my name, because you have shed so much blood before me upon the earth. Behold, a son shall be born to you; he shall be a man of peace. I will give him peace from all his enemies round about; for his name shall be Solomon (šᵉlōmô), and I will give peace (šālōm) and quiet (šeqeṭ) to Israel in his days. He shall build a house for my name." (1 Chr 22:8–10 RSV)

As evidence of the consistency with which the Chronicler has applied this concept, it should be noted that he has removed both occurrences of forms of *nûaḥ*, "rest," from his account of the dynastic oracle to David in 2 Samuel 7 which he has otherwise largely repeated in 1 Chronicles 17. The opening verse is simply altered to read, "Now when David dwelt in his house, David said . . ." (1 Chr 17:1; cf. 2 Sam

The Promised Rest

7:1). And the troublesome "I will/have given rest" of 2 Samuel 7:11 is simply altered to "I will *subdue* (Heb. root *kn'*) all your enemies" (1 Chr 17:10). Thus the writer has removed both the promise of and the reality of rest from the reign of David, since such rest is for him the prerequisite for the building of the temple. Solomon is the chosen temple builder, as is shown by the fact that he enjoyed a rest which his father David did not.

Three further developments in the concept of rest need to be mentioned. First, with the temple completed and Israel at rest in its land, the temple itself becomes the resting place of Yahweh.

> Then King David rose to his feet and said, "Hear me, my brethren and my people. I had it in my heart to build a *house of rest* for the ark of the covenant of Yahweh and for the footstool of our God; and I made preparations for building. (1 Chr 28:2 RSV, italics added)

It is therefore fitting that, at the end of Solomon's dedicatory prayer, the contents of 1 Kings 8:50b–51 are omitted in favor of a quotation from Psalms 132:8–9. The passage in Kings mentions God's activity for Israel in the Exodus.

> "And now arise, O Yahweh God,
> and go to thy resting place,
> thou and the ark of thy might.
> Let thy priests, O Yahweh God, be clothed with
> salvation,
> and let thy saints rejoice in thy goodness.
> O Yahweh God, do not turn away the face of thy
> anointed one!
> Remember thy steadfast love for David thy servant."
> (2 Chr 6:41–42 RSV)

With the statements that "the glory of Yahweh filled the temple" (2 Chr 7:1) and "the glory of Yahweh filled Yahweh's house" (2 Chr 7:2), Solomon's prayer is certainly pictured as answered. With Israel at rest in its land, and the temple erected, God himself takes up his rest among his people in his house.

Secondly, other kings in particular favor with the Chronicler are said to have enjoyed rest as a sign of the prosperity which marked their reigns. (See pp. 84–85.) This is true of Asa (2 Chr 14:5; 15), Jehoshaphat (2 Chr 20:30), and Hezekiah (2 Chr 32:22).* Any reference to rest is surprisingly absent from the account of Josiah's reign, where the signs of prosperity are restricted to religious reforms.

Finally, attention might be directed to the New Testament, which continues the concept of a divinely granted rest. Jesus, for example, invited those who heard him to come to him and experience the rest which he offered:

"Come to me, all who labor and are heavy laden, and I will give you rest. Take my yoke upon you, and learn from me; for I am gentle and lowly in heart, and you will find rest for your souls. For my yoke is easy, and my burden is light." (Matt 11:28–30 RSV)

Here the rest offered by Jesus to those accepting him is paralleled with the easy yoke and the light burden, and would stand in contrast to the heavy burdens associated with the legalism of the Pharisees.

The book of Hebrews resumes the concept of a divinely provided rest in a promised land, and raises it to a higher key. Moses and many of those who left Egypt with him were unable to enter the promised land because of their unbelief,

---

* 2 Chronicles 32:22 reads *wayyānah*, in the Hebrew, as suggested by the Septuagint and Vulgate, instead of *way'naḥălēm*.

the Hebrews writer argues (Heb 3:11-18). That means that the promise still remains, since God can surely not be unfaithful: "So then, there remains a sabbath rest for the people of God" (Heb 4:9).

To a people facing religious assimilation, as were perhaps the Israelites of the Chronicler's day—to a people facing religious persecution, as were perhaps those to whom Hebrews was written—to all people in all ages—the message remains the same. "Let us therefore strive to enter that rest" . . . (Heb 4:11). The God of the fathers still speaks to his people through his Word, and that Word of God is still "living and active" (Heb 4:12). Those who hear must not refuse to hearken to his voice, but must "draw near with a true heart in full assurance of faith" and thus enter into the heavenly rest (Heb 10:19, 22). The great crowd of witnesses throughout the ages encourages us as we seek to overcome the trials that are before us (Heb 12:1).

Summary

The themes we have met in the books of Chronicles are generally not unique to it. Topics such as the kingdom of God, Israel, the temple, the Word of God, and divine retribution are at the very center of the Old Testament revelation. Nevertheless, standing firmly in the line of Old Testament tradition, the Chronicler emphasizes some items and minimizes others as he thinks best to bring the Word of God to bear upon the particular circumstances of his day.

Since the Chronicler judged the temple to be of central importance for his day, he has stressed the importance of Solomon, who built the temple. Doubtless to protect the reputation of Solomon the temple builder, he removed all signs of misconduct from the reign of that king. It was not

Solomon the temple builder who was responsible for the division of the kingdom, but others who followed after him.

Though the temple may be a significant symbol for the writer, it must be said that it is also much more than that. The temple is the place where one normally draws closest to God. It is the place where God's praises are chanted, where sacrifices are offered to his name, where priests and Levites lead the people in offering the devotion and praise that spring from a pure and thankful heart. It is difficult even today to find fault with such a perception.

Modern readers are apt to be disturbed by Chronicles' presentation of the dogma of retribution, which seems so rigid and contrary to human experience. This is a subject, it should be noted, which was troublesome already in Old Testament books, such as Ezekiel and Job, where it was generally found wanting. But to the Chronicler's credit it ought to be noted that concepts such as mercy and repentance, which, strictly speaking, have no place in a rigid understanding of retribution, are all-important parts of his theology. It is still difficult for us to rise to that level of understanding.

In other areas too, Chronicles shows itself to possess a positive and sensitive understanding of the ways of God and people. Contrary no doubt to the popular feelings of his day, he continued to view inhabitants of the land previously occupied by the northern tribes as brothers, and fought energetically to see that others did so also. Ultimately he viewed faith in Yahweh, which admittedly expressed itself in support of and worship at the Jerusalem temple, as the only thing that mattered in one's relationship to God. He knew that faithfulness, mercy, purity of heart, unaffected joy, and cheerful generosity were marks of those who possessed that faith.

To that end he set himself about the task of considering the Word of God which he had received, and applying it to himself and the people of his day. We may not know exactly how that word was received in his or other days. But to this day those who apply themselves sympathetically to his message and his methods still have God's promise spoken through a better-known and perhaps more conventional prophet, that his word will not return void, but will accomplish that for which it was purposed.

NOTES

Introduction
1. See R. Braun, *1 Chronicles*, Word Biblical Commentary, vol. 14 (Waco, Tex.: Word, 1986), xxviii–xxix, for a summary of positions held.

Chapter 2   The Temple
1. While debate concerning the variant readings in this most important chapter has been profuse, it appears that the differences are insignificant. Cf. WBC 14, 195–200. While less polemically so, it was clear already in the mind of DH also that it was actually Solomon who built the temple.

2. See R. Braun, "Solomon, the Chosen Temple Builder: The Significance of 1 Chronicles 22, 28, and 29 for the Theology of Chronicles," *Journal of Biblical Literature* 95 (1976):581–90, for a detailed exposition of these points.

3. R. B. Dillard, *2 Chronicles*, WBC 15 (Waco, Tex.: Word, 1987), 4–5, has demonstrated that Chronicles' figure of Huram is modeled upon the craftsman of the tabernacle in Exodus 31 and 35, Oholiab.

4. On seeking Yahweh, see p. 81; on repentance in Chronicles, p. 100.

Chapter 3 The Kingdom of God

1. J. Wellhausen, *Prolegomena to the History of Ancient Israel* (New York: Meridian Books, 1957), 182.

2. G. von Rad, *Das Geschichtsbild des chronistischen Werkes* (Stuttgart: W. Kohlhammer, 1930).

3. In such close proximity it is possible that the reference to Hezekiah's action in stationing the Levites in the temple with certain instruments "according to the commandment of David and of Gad the king's seer and of Nathan the prophet" (2 Chr 29:25) may refer as much to the musical instruments involved as to the installation of the Levites, although it is impossible to be certain.

4. See R. Braun, "Solomonic Apologetic," *Journal of Biblical Literature* 92 (1973):503-16, especially p. 512. In the original account of Kings, Jeroboam first returned to Israel in 1 Kings 12:20. Note the present unevenness between 1 Kings 12:2-3a and verse 20.

Chapter 4 The People of God: All Israel

1. See R. Braun, "The Significance of 1 Chronicles 22, 28, and 29 for the Structure and Theology of the Work of the Chronicler" (Diss. Concordia Seminary, St. Louis, 1971), 190, for the justification of this translation.

2. W. Rudolph, *Chronikbücher*, Handbuch zum Alten Testament (Tübingen: Mohr, 1965), xxi, 291.

3. See R. J. Coggins, *Samaritans and Jews: The Origins of Samaritanism Reconsidered* (Atlanta: John Knox, 1975), and the many references there.

4. See R. Braun, "A Reconsideration of the Chronicler's Attitude Toward the North," *Journal of Biblical Literature* 96 (1977): 59-62. The apostle Paul pursues the nature of the true Israel further in Romans 9-11, modeled upon the premise that "all Israel will be saved."

Chapter 6 Divine Retribution

1. Cf. Jehoshaphat, 2 Chronicles 17:3; Hezekiah, 2 Chronicles 29:3, 32:4; Josiah, 2 Chronicles 34:3; and contrast 2 Kings 22:3.

2. Cf. R. Braun, "2 Chronicles," *Harper's Bible Commentary*, ed. J. L. Mayes (San Francisco: Harper and Row, 1988), especially pp. 363-71.

3. Concerning Hezekiah's reign, see H. G. M. Williamson, *Israel in the Books of Chronicles* (Cambridge: Cambridge University Press, 1977), 119–31; R. B. Dillard, *2 Chronicles*, WBC 15:226–61.

4. On this literary form see R. Braun, *1 Chronicles*, WBC 14:221–25.

5. See R. Braun, "Chronicles, Ezra, and Nehemiah: Theology and Literary History," *Supplement to Vetus Testamentum* 30 (1979): 52–64, for additional evidence.

Chapter 9   The Promised Rest

1. It is probably the writer's inconsistency in the use of the concept of rest that has resulted in divergent translations of the perfect verb forms with prefixed *waw* ("and") in verses 9b–11 as either past or future, including the "I will give/have given you rest" in verse 11. For discussion, see *1 Chronicles*, WBC 14: 198–99.

BIBLIOGRAPHY

Ackroyd, P. *I and II Chronicles, Ezra, Nehemiah.* Torch Bible Commentary. London: SCM Press, 1973.

Braun, R. L. *1 Chronicles.* Word Biblical Commentary, vol. 14. Waco, Tex.: Word, 1986.

————. "A Reconsideration of the Chronicler's Attitude Toward the North," *Journal of Biblical Literature* 96 (1977): 59–62.

————. "Chronicles, Ezra, and Nehemiah: Theology and Literary History," *Supplement to Vetus Testamentum* 30 (1979): 52–64.

————. "1 Chronicles," "2 Chronicles," *Harper's Bible Commentary,* James Mayes, ed. San Francisco: Harper and Row, 1988, 342–71.

————. "Solomonic Apologetic in Chronicles." *Journal of Biblical Literature* 92 (1973): 503–16.

————. "Solomon, the Chosen Temple Builder: The Significance of 1 Chronciles 22, 28, and 29 for the Theology of Chronicles," *Journal of Biblical Literature* 95 (1976): 581–90.

Coggins, R. J. *The First and Second Books of Chronicles.* Cambridge Bible Commentary on the New English Bible. Cambridge: Cambridge University Press, 1976.

————. *The Origins of Samaritanism Reconsidered.* Atlanta: John Knox, 1975.

Cross, F. M. "A Reconstruction of the Judean Restoration," *Journal of Biblical Literature* 94 (1975): 4–18.

Dillard, R. B. *2 Chronicles.* Word Biblical Commentary, vol. 15. Waco, Tex.: Word, 1987.

Japhet, S. "The Supposed Common Authorship of Chronicles and Ezra-Nehemiah Investigated Anew," *Vetus Testamentum* 18 (1968): 330–71.

Lemke, W. E. "The Synoptic Problem in the Chronicler's History," *Harvard Theological Review* 58 (1965): 349–63.

McKenzie, S. L. *The Chronicler's Use of the Deuteronomic History.* Harvard Semitic Monographs 33. Atlanta: Scholars Press, 1984.

Myers, J. M. *1 Chronicles.* Anchor Bible, vol. 12. Garden City, N.Y.: Doubleday, 1965.

————. *2 Chronicles.* Anchor Bible, vol. 13. Garden City, N.Y.: Doubleday, 1965.

Newsome, J. D. "Toward a New Understanding of the Chronicler and His Purposes," *Journal of Biblical Literature* 94 (1975): 201–17.

Petersen, D. L. *Late Israelite Prophecy.* Studies in Deutero-Prophetic Literature and in Chronicles. SBL Monograph Series 23. Missoula: Scholars Press, 1977.

Throntveit, M. A. *When Kings Speak.* Royal Speech and Royal Prayer in Chronicles. SBL Dissertation Series 93. Atlanta: Scholars Press, 1987.

Welch, A. C. *The Work of the Chronicler.* London: Oxford University Press, 1939.

Williamson, H. G. M. *1 and 2 Chronicles.* New Century Bible Commentary. London: Marshall, Morgan, and Scott, 1982.

————. *Israel in the Books of Chronicles.* Cambridge: Cambridge University Press, 1977.

————. "The Accession of Solomon in the Books of Chronicles." *Vetus Testamentum* 26 (1976): 351–61.

INDEX OF SCRIPTURE PASSAGES

Index of Scriptures

8 2-6	86	14 1-2	85	19 8	61
8 12-15	14	14·3	72, 81	19 9	92
8 12-16	40, 65	14 4	50	20 1-30	86
8 14	18, 32-33	14 5	111	20 3-4	82
8 16	14, 40	14 6	83, 86	20 5	64
8 29	18	14 6-7	72	20·6-12	15
9 1-31	14	14·7	50, 70	20 14-17	64
9 23	86	14.8	86	20 15-17	15
10-36	6, 51	14 10	82	20 17	84
10 1	50	14 12-15	86	20 20	82-83
10 15	42	14 15	111	20 29	86
10 17	50	14 5-7	85	20.30	85, 111
10:19	42	15	52	20·34	63
10 22	85	15·1-7	63, 64	20.37	63, 82
11.1-3	7	15.2	50, 70	21 6	88
11.4-9	7	15 2-7	72	21:10	87
11 5-12	71, 86	15 4	3, 101	21·12	63
11 13-15	14	15.8	51-52, 72, 86	21 14	88
11 16	14, 51	15 8-9	50	21·18	88
11 17	34, 41, 71, 85	15 8-15	15	22 1	12
11 18-21	71	15 8-18	73	22 8	31
11 22-23	71	15:9	52, 73, 84	22·9	92
12 1	61, 70, 87	15·11	52	22:11-12	15
12 2	70	15:12	81, 92	23	18
12:5	63, 70, 87	15.12-13	82	23 1-21	15
12 6-7	65	15 13	3, 52, 73	23 18	32, 61, 94
12:6-8	101	15 15	73, 94	23:18-21	62
12:6-12	100	15.17	73, 92	24·4	86
12 7	63, 89	16 7	70, 82	24 4-14	16
12:9-11	101	16 7-8	82	24 5-6	50
12 12	71, 89, 101	16.7-9	63	24 9	62
12 14	81	16.9	88	24.10	94
13	14, 42, 87	16.10	74	24.18	3, 16, 87
13 3	86	16 12	74, 88	24:20	83
13 4	25, 50	16 38	92	24.20-22	64
13 5	3, 33, 44, 50, 54	17:1	85	24 23-24	16, 88
13:8	25, 42, 54	17·2	51	24:24	3
13·9	42, 88	17 3	82, 84, 116n	24 25	88
13 9-11	15	17:3-19	86	25 4	61
13 9-12	88	17 4	82	25.7-9	63
13 10-11	42	17:5	85	25.11-13	86
13 10-12	20	17 9	61-62	25.15	82
13 11	88	17 10	86	25 15-16	63
13 12	42, 83-84, 89	17 11	85-86	25 17-24	88
13 13-20	86	17 12	86	25 20	82
13 15	50	18	63	25:24	16
13·18	43, 50, 54, 71, 82	19 1-3	63	25 27	88
13·19	51	19.2	89	26 5	83
13 19-22	71	19.3	89	26.6-8	86
13.21	85	19 6	84	26:6-15	75

1, 2 CHRONICLES